Robert W. Catsburg

FIVE DAYS IN NOVEMBER

The liberation of Welberg and Steenbergen in WWII

Edited and translated by Ineke Hardy

Originally published in the Netherlands as

Vijf dagen in November.
De bevrijding van Welberg en Steenbergen in de tweede wereldoorlog
by the *De Steenen Kamer* Historical Society, Steenbergen, 2009

Printed in Canada
Volumes Publishing

Cover drawing: Major G.L. Cassidy, DSO,
courtesy of Joan McKinnon née Stirling
Cover design: Marion Freymann
Cover layout: Kevin Strang, courtesy of Lynn Johnston
Interior design: Ineke Hardy
Printed and bound in Canada

ISBN 978-0-9867354-0-0

We gratefully acknowledge the generous financial support of
the Embassy of the Kingdom of the Netherlands in Ottawa,
the family of Brig. Gen. Edward Amy, DSO, OBE, MC, CD,
the South Alberta Light Horse Regiment Foundation,
the Algonquin Regiment Association,
and the family of Major Keith Stirling.

Library and Archives Canada Cataloguing in Publication

Catsburg, Robert W.
    Five days in November : the liberation of Welberg and Steenbergen in World War II / Robert W.
Catsburg ; edited and translated by Ineke Hardy.

Translation of: Vijf dagen in november.
ISBN 978-0-9867354-0-0

    1. Canada. Canadian Army--History--World War, 1939-1945. 2. World War, 1939-1945--Campaigns
--Netherlands. 3. World War, 1939-1945--Netherlands. I. Hardy, Ineke II. Title.

D763.N42S7413 2010   940.54'21492   C2010-906790-8

DEDICATION

To the memory of Major Keith Stirling,

to all the veterans, dead and alive, who answered the call,

and to the Dutch civilians who died along with their liberators.

We will remember them.

Foreword

Brig. Gen. (ret'd) E.A.C. "Ned" Amy,
D.S.O., O.B.E., M.C., C.D.

Robert Catsburg kindly invited me to write a foreword to Ineke Hardy's English translation of his book *Five Days in November*. My memories of the civilian population in Holland in 1944/45 are of a brave people who had been subjected to extreme hardships under the Nazi occupation.

Regrettably, my recall of events which occurred during the five days of this action 66 years ago is, at best, sketchy. However, I wish to provide some observations, in the hope that readers may better understand the backgrounds of WWII Canadian soldiers who participated in that battle.

At the beginning of the Second World War, the actual size of the full-time "regular" Canadian Army was around 5,000 men. Not a large number. However, in addition to its full-time professionals, Canada had developed and maintained a very successful militia organization that provided the overwhelming majority of its soldiers, who came from hundreds of communities. It permitted Canada, with a population of twelve million, to recruit and train the hundreds of thousands of volunteers who fought overseas.

One will note the names of Canadian cities, provinces, and regions in the names of many of the units that fought during the actions described in this book. Many of the soldiers were from small communities similar in size to those of Steenbergen and Welberg. As civilians they may have been fishermen, farmers, loggers, miners, civil servants, clerks, professionals, salesmen, or from the ranks of the unemployed. They came from all walks of life, from all of Canada's diverse regions, from coast to coast. When they enlisted, they agreed at the outset to stay in the military "for the duration of the war". In September of 1939, no one knew how long that was going to be. All we knew is that the country had declared war against the Nazis, and we knew it was going to be a hard slog. For those who enlisted in 1939, many were not to see their families again for four years or more.

The war in Europe lasted 68 months, from September 1939 to May 1945. The battle for Steenbergen took place on the 62nd or 63rd month of the war, with six months remaining prior to Germany's unconditional surrender.

The German Army was well equipped and well trained for mechanized warfare. Canada's lessons learned on the battlefields were tough ones. In 1942 we first encountered German soldiers on the landing beach at Dieppe. Subsequent battles in Sicily and Italy in 1943 and 1944 provided further lessons from this skilled opponent, who possessed superior equipment.

A number of the Canadian soldiers who participated in the battles around Steenbergen had their first encounter with the German army in Italy. My close friend Major "Snuffy" Smith and I were two of those who were posted from the Italian theatre to Normandy in 1944. We joined our new regiment, the Canadian Grenadier Guards (22 CAR), as Squadron Commanders.

The liberation of North-West Europe had begun on the beaches of Normandy, roughly five months prior to the events described in *Five days in November*.

From the hedgerows to the polders, five months of engagement with the enemy had transformed the members of the 4th Canadian Armoured Division into experienced warriors. This, of course, equally applied to other Canadian units in the field in late 1944. The enemy fought tenaciously throughout that time period. By the time our soldiers had reached Steenbergen, they were veterans all. Many were buried on the battlefields of France, Belgium, and Holland. Of those present during the events in this book, many more would not survive the six months remaining of the war in Europe.

Measured in calendar months the liberation occurred rather quickly. However, for the soldiers on the battlefield, who finished one battle only to be confronted by yet another, it seemed that the war had been going on forever.

By the war's end, many Canadian families had not seen their loved ones for four years or more. All dreaded the telegram informing them that a family member had been wounded, killed, or was missing in action. During those difficult days in late 1944, civilians in both the Netherlands and in Canada had suffered terribly. The war was hell for all concerned.

Most of those young men who served and survived the war went back into civilian life upon returning home. They went on with their lives, raised families, and enjoyed their hard-won freedoms. They went overseas as boys and returned as men. Some of their great-grandchildren are fighting in Afghanistan against another tough enemy. It is to these we have thrown the torch.

The Canadian Army was the finest "band of brothers" a soldier could belong to. I am proud to have served with them and I am forever mindful of those who never made it home and "who shall remain forever young" in the Canadian and Commonwealth War Cemeteries scattered across the landscapes of Italy, France, Belgium, and the Netherlands. Though my memory may fail me on the specifics of particular battles, I shall never forget my comrades and my friends.

I am sure the people from the Welberg-Steenbergen area will recognize the place names mentioned, and they will value this work as an important contribution to their regional history. It was no doubt a challenge for the author to flesh out events that occurred 66 years ago through the piecing together of records from regimental war diaries, overly folded maps, and citations.

The observations of the Dutch child witnesses cited in *Five Days in November* provide an important contribution to understanding the hardships endured by the soldiers and civilians alike.

We Canadians are touched by the kindness shown to us by the Dutch people. We are grateful that they remember us as liberators, and that they continue to honour our fallen soldiers. I congratulate the author, Robert Catsburg, and translator, Ineke Hardy, for a job well done.

Halifax, Nova Scotia, Canada,
August 16, 2010

The publication before you is the story of the battles fought to liberate Welberg and Steenbergen in November 1944. At the time of writing, it was 65 years ago that these events took place, and the time left to the generation that consciously experienced the war is running out. This document, therefore, attempts to preserve the details of this episode for the benefit of future generations.

The central part of this work is based on information from Canadian regimental histories. Many of these books were produced shortly after the end of the war, as a memento for the soldiers returning home. They contain a wealth of information relating to both military operations and personal experiences of Canadian soldiers. Additional sources used are the personal memoirs of several Canadian veterans and archival documentation from Ottawa. All this material has been interwoven with the experiences of local residents. Interviews were conducted with close to a dozen residents of Welberg who witnessed the battles. The author hopes that this approach will provide the reader with a balanced depiction of the battle, viewed from the perspective of the Canadian soldiers as well as that of the local population.

Since it is becoming increasingly difficult to communicate with residents who were adults during the war, it was decided to interview people who were children at that time. Most of that generation experienced the war as an exciting time, filled with adventure. Their experiences were less intense, more light-hearted, and above all, less emotionally charged than those of the older generation. This proved to be a major advantage to the author. People were very candid and spoke easily of the events in their past. The old adage "little pitchers have big ears" worked very much to the author's benefit.

To guide the reader, the following summarizes the organization of the material: preceded by an introduction setting out the events leading up to the battle of Steenbergen, the story is presented on a day-by-day basis. The format resembles that of a diary. The course of the battle is described by front sector (Welbergsedijk, Welberg, Waterhoefke, Kladde/Glymes, etc.). With each change of front sector, the day starts over again, as it occurred during the battle. The appendix contains a list of abbreviations and details of relevant military and technical information. The numbers enclosed in square brackets found in the text refer to the (numbered) list of sources consulted (pp. 136-139).

The author would like to take this opportunity to express his sincere gratitude to all those who were kind enough to contribute to the making of this book. Special thanks are due to Adri Helmons, who introduced the author to his extensive circle of friends and acquaintances. Many of the photographs of Steenbergen used in this book are courtesy of Piet Adriaansen. Con Slokkers was kind enough to review the manuscript to check it for errors. Finally, the author is indebted to Johan van Doorn for his kind permission to use a number of archival documents and for his constructive criticism.

This publication is specially dedicated to the Canadian soldiers who put their lives on the line to liberate us. The author hopes that those who read this text will be motivated to pay a visit to the soldiers who are buried in the war cemetery in Bergen op Zoom.

Should any part of this publication be in need of correction or if essential information is found to be missing, the author and/or translator would appreciate hearing from you. They can be contacted at <r.w.catsburg@gmail.com> or <ihstranslations@rogers.com>.

In the summer of 2008, on my return from my vacation, I was greeted by my friend Ad Helmons, who handed me a small cross. It was the sort of cross you find in all war cemeteries in western Europe, made of plain wood and adorned by a plastic poppy. Someone had left it in a flower pot in the Cornelius Church in Welberg and inscribed it with the words: "Major Stirling, captured in Welberg, 1 November 1944." It seemed logical to assume that this was the work of a member of the Major's family, and I immediately set out trying to contact these people, anxious to obtain personal information and photos of the man who played such an important part in the battle of Welberg. Following a telephone call to the president of the Regimental Association of the Algonquins in North Bay (Col. John Smith), I soon received a call from Mrs Sandra O'Grady née Stirling, one of the Major's daughters. In the course of our conversation, we found that we shared an enthusiastic interest in the events that took place in Welberg on 1 November 1944. Mrs O'Grady was kind enough to give me access to her father's diary, which proved to be a precious source of information regarding the battle of Welberg. This unique material, in combination with the insatiable hunger for information on my part and that of my friend Ad Helmons, made me decide to embark on a detailed study of the battle of Welberg.

From the start, I knew that I wanted to bring back to life not only the military tactical situation but also the human aspects. Since my fascination with our Canadian liberators has been with me since my early childhood, I was well equipped to construct a solid account of the military events. As to the stories of the people who witnessed the events, I am indebted to Ad Helmons, who has been and continues to be my "spy." Ad, born and bred in Welberg, knows everyone and he introduced me to the people who were in a position to contribute to the book. Since neither I nor my family are native to the village, people felt free to speak openly of this eventful and emotional period. The book then took shape with the support of the historical society of Steenbergen. The society's publishing experience and interest in the greater good of Steenbergen were strong arguments to team up with them to launch the book. The first print run sold out within weeks and the second one within a few months. A total of 450 copies of the Dutch version are in circulation.

It goes without saying that a number of copies of the Dutch edition were sent to Canadian friends. At the time, I dismissed the language barrier by telling them to get help from a Dutch-speaking friend or neighbour. Not in my wildest dreams did I dare hope to see the book published in Canada one day. I lack the skills to translate the text into proper English and I could not imagine that there would be sufficient interest in the book. It was Sandy O'Grady, fascinated with the blend of civilian and military accounts and anecdotes contained in the book, who conceived the translation project and launched it with spirit and enthusiasm. It was Sandy who found our translator, Ineke Hardy, in Ottawa. Ineke, a professional translator whose grandparents spent the war in a small town 50 km from Welberg, immediately volunteered her services and embraced the project, translating and editing the book with passion and love. Following Sandy O'Grady's visit to Welberg, Ineke came to Welberg herself to see the place where it all happened, guided by myself and Ad Helmons. I think it is no exaggeration to state that Ineke and Sandy have done a fantastic job.

In conclusion, I would like to say that the Canadian version of *Five days in November* exceeds my wildest dreams. As a child, while still in elementary school, I used to play "museum" in my room. Now I have been given the opportunity to commemorate our liberators in a timeless fashion and in their own language. I hope the book will go some way towards paying off the debt we Dutch people owe to countless families in Canada.

Editor's note

Accounts of military operations, especially those conducted in an urban setting, inevitably involve geographical references and street names. In its original concept, "Five Days in November" was intended primarily for the residents of the Steenbergen/Welberg region and thus, for a readership intimately familiar with local urban and geographical features. Names of streets, canals, rivers, dikes, polders, ponds, and other landmarks aided readers in understanding the course of the various engagements that took place. This, of course, is not the case for Canadian readers with no or limited knowledge of the area. It was a problem that required editorial intervention. Translating proper nouns is a practice translators prefer to avoid, except in the case of a translation in general use, such as "Munich" for "München." In consultation with the author, it was therefore decided to retain the Dutch names and add two maps: one of the greater Steenbergen region, and one a larger-scale map of the towns of Steenbergen and Welberg. This will permit readers to orient themselves and follow the course of the battles as they unfold in the book. Map coordinates have been provided whenever possible and qualifiers have been added to names that might lead to confusion. Roads running along the top of dikes, for instance, often carry the same name as the dikes themselves. Thus, "Groenedijk" (Green Dike) refers to both the dike and the road that follows its course. References to dike roads will, therefore, be in the form of "Groenedijk road." Unless otherwise specified, map coordinates refer to map III on p. 9. In addition, Appendix I (p. 104) presents an alphabetical list of names with map coordinates and brief descriptions, and a list of the most common Dutch words denoting "street" and "waterway." It is hoped that this information will help guide readers through the labyrinth of Dutch names. For those wishing more information about the locations mentioned, Google Maps (http://maps.google.com/) will take them there.

Editorial intervention has been kept to a minimum. Here and there, a few details were added for the sake of clarity. A brief description of the area was added on p. 8, the bibliography was worked out in more detail, a list of maps was added, as were a few photos, an additional map (p. 8), and an index of names of persons. Appendix I was expanded, and the account of the van Hooijdonk family on p. 79 ff. was added at the author's suggestion. The photo on p. 77 replaces a photo of Dutch O.D. members. A few paragraphs in the final section were slightly amended. The excerpts from Canadian war diaries were reprinted without emendations to retain the flavour of these accounts. The list of casualties on pp. 122/123 was expanded with the hometown of each fallen soldier as far as this could be ascertained. It may be of interest to the families of these men to know that their records can be obtained from Library and Archives Canada at http://www.collectionscanada.gc.ca/databases/war-dead/. Details are also available from the Commonwealth War Graves Commission at http://www.cwgc.org/.

Brigadier-General (ret'd) Edward Amy DSO, OBE, MC, CD, aged 92, graciously agreed to provide a foreword. Thanks are due to his son Michael for his assistance. We are also grateful for the support of Susan Angus of the South Alberta Light Horse Regiment Foundation. Major Stirling's granddaughter Marion Freymann created the cover design, based on a drawing by Major G.L. Cassidy originally owned by Major Stirling. Permission to reprint the drawing was kindly granted by Major Stirling's daughter Joan McKinnon. As a point of interest, author Robert Catsburg owns and occupies the house that is partly visible in the lower right-hand corner of this drawing. Cartoonist Lynn Johnston of "For Better of For Worse" fame was kind enough to offer the services of graphic artist Kevin Strang for the cover layout. Many thanks are due to

Major Colin Michaud and my husband, Major (ret'd) Daniel Stovel, who proofread the manuscript and whose informed comments and eye for detail greatly enhanced the final version of this book. Any translation errors are solely my responsibility. My husband and my son, Daniel Hardy, another retired Army officer, patiently explained the intricacies of warfare, armoured vehicles, artillery fire, and all the other equipment and procedures that were part of the arsenal of the Canadian army in WWII. Author Robert Catsburg and his associate, Mr Ad Helmons, took me on a guided tour of the Welberg area so I could see for myself where it all happened.

This publication would not have been possible without the generous support of the Embassy of the Kingdom of the Netherlands, the South Alberta Light Horse Regiment Foundation, the Algonquin Regiment Association, the family of Major Keith Stirling, and the family of Brig. Gen. (ret'd) "Ned" Amy, and without the initiative of Sandra "Sandy" O'Grady née Stirling, who launched the project, encouraged by history teacher John Hetherington of North Bay. As for me, born in the Netherlands near the end of the war, it has been a privilege to work on this project, to which I have donated a major portion of my services.

Table of contents

Foreword by Brig. Gen. (ret'd) E.A.C. "Ned" Amy, DSO, OBE, MC, CD i

Author's note to the Dutch edition iv

Author's note to the Canadian edition vi

Editor's note viii

Table of contents x

Prelude 1

The Allied advance in September and October 1944 2

The German defence 8

Sunday 29 October 1944 17

Monday 30 October 1944 21

Tuesday 31 October 1944 29

Wednesday 1 November 1944 43

Thursday 2 November 1944 50

Friday 3 November 1944 61

Saturday 4 November 1944 74

Sunday 5 November 1944 85

The winter months 88

The civilian situation after the liberation 93

Casualties among the civilian population of the town of Steenbergen ... 97

Looking back on the battles in Steenbergen 100

Appendices

    I.   Names, terms, and abbreviations 104

    II.   The Fourth Canadian Armoured Division 108

    III. War monuments in and near Steenbergen 120

    IV. Canadian casualties in the battles of Welberg and Steenbergen ... 122

    V.   German casualties of the battle of Steenbergen 128

    VI. Decorations awarded to Canadian soldiers in the battle of Steenbergen ... 129

    VII. Sources consulted 138

    VIII. List of maps 142

Index of names of persons 143

"It seemed as though a massive thunderstorm were raging over the city of Bergen op Zoom. Continuous, heavy rumbling was heard from that direction and at night, the sky lit up as if cleaved by bolts of lightning. From the beginning of October onwards, we heard it come ever closer."

That, in the words of Welberg resident Ad Helmons, was how the war announced itself to the residents of Steenbergen and surroundings. Despite assurances from "the bride"[1] that the region would be spared the ravages of war, few people were willing to take a chance and most went to work digging a shelter in their backyards. This usually took the form of a wide trench covered with logs, buried under a layer of soil up to half a metre thick. Few residents realized at that point that they would be forced to spend endless hours in these primitive shelters, enduring appalling conditions in a desperate battle to survive ...

---

[1] The "bride of Steenbergen" was a widely known Roman Catholic medium and stigmatic by the name of Janske Gorissen. Active from 1929 to 1951, this alleged manifestation of the Holy Virgin drew pilgrims from all over the Netherlands and even Belgium, and inspired a cult of intense Marian devotion in Welberg. In 1951, the church officially rejected the alleged medium's claims and put an end to the cult.

The Allied advance in September and October 1944

The following chapter presents a brief overview of the advance of the British / Canadian forces from the landing beaches in Normandy to Antwerp. For more detailed information, readers are referred to Appendix VII (Sources consulted).

The landing in Normandy

On 6 June, 1944, the Allied Expeditionary Force carried out a successful landing on the beaches of Normandy. American, Canadian, British, and French troops came ashore along a stretch of coastline many kilometres long. While the British and Canadians tied up the main German forces near Caen, the Americans broke through the German lines to the south, near Argentan. The Allies then entrapped the enemy by carrying out a so-called pincer movement near the town of Falaise. The Germans found themselves under attack from the British and the Canadians from the west and the Americans from the east. Following the destruction of the bulk of the German forces west of the river Seine, it took the Allies only a few weeks to advance past Brussels.

The Canadians were assigned to the left flank of the Allied advance during this phase. Crossing the Seine, they captured the fortress towns of Boulogne and Calais by the end of September. Due to supply problems, widespread fatigue, and unexpected German resistance, this advance came to a halt near Bruges and Ghent.

The importance of Antwerp

The British XXX Corps, operating east of the 2nd Canadian Corps, liberated Antwerp in early September 1944. The port facilities, essential to a successful continuation of the campaign to bring Germany to its knees, fell into Allied hands intact. Despite the capture of Antwerp, however, German control of the Scheldt estuary prevented Allied ships from delivering supplies. Every litre of gasoline, every bullet, and all the needs of a fighting army had to be transported to the front from far-away Normandy, and this long supply line was seriously hampering the campaign. Field Marshall Montgomery, commander of the British and Canadian forces (21st Army Group), assigned top priority to an attack on the Ruhr Region, intending to cross the Meuse and the Rhine at Nijmegen and Arnhem and defeat Germany before the onset of winter. This operation, code-named "Market Garden," led to the disastrous Battle of Arnhem. Montgomery saw the opening of the Antwerp port as a lower priority because he fully expected the Canadian army to be able to clear the banks of the Scheldt. Montgomery's superior (General Eisenhower), however, was acutely aware of the strategic importance of Antwerp, and the difference of opinion between the two men eventually led to conflict. Montgomery backed down and in mid October, the available supplies, although limited, were turned over to the Canadian army on the left flank.

The Germans rally after their flight from France

After being surrounded at Falaise, the Germans were forced into a chaotic retreat towards Antwerp, and the German 15th Army found itself boxed in between Antwerp and the Belgian coast. As the idea of breaking out to the east through the Allied lines was judged unrealistic, the remnants of this army were ferried across the Western Scheldt.

General Kurt Chill, disregarding orders to return to Germany, personally initiated the formation of a defensive line composed of hastily assembled troops behind the Albert Canal. Another improvised line of defence was set up in West Flanders, behind the Leopold Canal. Contrary to all expectations, the Germans succeeded in putting a temporary halt to the advance of the 2nd Canadian Corps, although they lost Eastern Zeeland Flanders following a push by the 1st Polish Armoured Division. Thanks to the bold action of the German army command, the 15th German Army was eventually rescued with relatively minor losses. The main force crossed the Scheldt at Breskens. After escaping the encirclement, this German army was deployed in western and central Brabant and played a major role in the Allied defeat at the Battle of Arnhem.

The Battle of the Scheldt

The German defenders took full advantage of the Allied pause. They hastily reinforced their defensive positions in preparation for the inevitable attack and brought in reinforcements. Well aware that the port of Antwerp was of little use to the Allies as long as the banks of the Scheldt remained in German hands, they ordered their troops to defend the most strategically important sectors (Walcheren, Western Zeeland Flanders, and the isthmus connecting South Beveland with Brabant) in the usual fashion: to the last man and to the last bullet.

The Allies also made preparations for the coming battle. The summary below lists the Allied units that engaged in battle with the Germans on the western flank, from the Channel coast to Breda. In addition, specialized units of the 34th British Armoured Brigade, the 2nd Canadian Armoured Brigade, and the 79th British Armoured Division were ready to be deployed on the front as needed.

First Canadian Army (Lieutenant General Harry Crerar)

II Canadian Corps (Lieutenant General Guy Simonds)

*	3rd Canadian Infantry Division	Western Zeeland Flanders (Operation Switchback - 6 Oct. 1944)
*	2nd Canadian Infantry Division	Woensdrecht, South Beveland
*	52nd (Lowland) Infantry Division	Vlissingen and South Beveland (Operations Infatuate and Vitality - 1 Nov./23 Oct. 1944) Westkapelle and Vlissingen
*	4th Special Service Brigade	(Operation Infatuate - 1 Nov. 1944)

I British Corps (Lieutenant-General John Crocker)

*	49th (West Riding) Infantry Division	Nispen, Roosendaal and eventually Willemstad
*	1st Polish Armoured Division	Breda, Wagenberg, Lage Zwaluwe and eventually Moerdijk
*	4th Canadian Armoured Division	Essen, Wouwse Plantage, Bergen op Zoom, Steenbergen (Operation Suitcase – 20 Oct. 1944)
*	104th American Infantry Division	Zundert, Oudenbosch, Standaardbuiten, Moerdijk

---

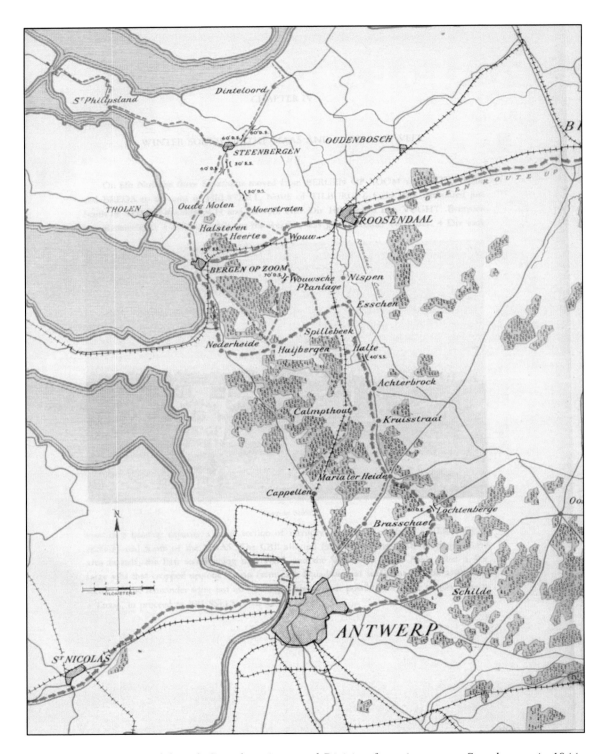

Map I: *The advance of the 4th Canadian Armoured Division from Antwerp to Steenbergen in 1944. The map was copied from* Green Route Up *[16].*

The plan for the 2nd Canadian Corps was to liberate Western Zeeland Flanders using the 3rd Canadian Infantry Division. The attack took place across the Leopold Canal and by means of an amphibian attack across the Braakman Inlet (Operation "Switchback"). The Commandos and Scots of the 52nd Division were assigned to liberate Walcheren (Operation "Infatuate") and to carry out an amphibious landing in South Beveland (Operation "Vitality"). Prior to this attack, the dikes in Walcheren were bombed, causing the island to flood. The 4th Canadian Armoured Division had no offensive assignment and was ordered to defend the line south of the Leopold Canal [20].

To dislodge the German defenders south of the Meuse river, the Allies conducted a three-pronged assault. The First British Corps, positioned north and east of Antwerp, was ordered to push north, the Polar Bears (the 49th West Riding Division) was to advance to Roosendaal, and the 1st Polish Armoured Division was to head for Breda. On 24 October, the American 104th Infantry Division (the Timberwolves) was assigned to the First British Corps to reinforce its push to the north. They were positioned between the 49th British Division and the 1st Polish Division. The 2nd Canadian Corps, positioned to the West, tasked the 2nd Canadian Infantry Division with sealing off the isthmus of South Beveland at Woensdrecht, after which it had orders to advance towards the Sloe dam together with the 52nd British Division.

The British XII Corps, finally, commanded by the British 2nd Army, was positioned in the corridor leading from Eindhoven to Nijmegen. On 16 October, this Corps was ordered to advance to the west at the same time as II Canadian Corps was launching its attack (Operation "Pheasant"). For the second time, the 15th German Army risked being encircled: from the south by the British I Corps, from the east by the British XII Corps, and to the west, in the Scheldt Estuary, by II Canadian Corps [2].

Composition of the 4th Canadian Armoured Division

Headquarters 4th Armoured Division...
       15th and 23rd (SP) Field Regiment, Royal Canadian Artillery
       8th and 9th Field Squadron, Royal Canadian Engineers
       Other support troops (Engineers, Medical Branch, Service Corps, etc.)

Headquarters 4th Armoured Brigade..
       21st Canadian Armoured Regiment (Governor General's Foot Guards)
       22nd Canadian Armoured Regiment (Canadian Grenadier Guards)
       28th Canadian Armoured Regiment (British Columbia Regiment)
       Lake Superior Regiment (Motor)

Headquarters 10th Infantry Brigade..
       29th Canadian Armoured Reconnaissance Regiment (South Alberta Regiment)
       Lincoln and Welland Regiment
       Algonquin Regiment
       Argyll and Sutherland Highlanders of Canada
       10th Independent Machine Gun Company (New Brunswick Rangers)

(See Appendix II for a detailed description of this Division)

The attack stalls at Woensdrecht

The attack in the 1st Canadian Army's sector was launched in early October along the entire front (i.e. from Zeeland Flanders through to Antwerp) and did not proceed according to plan. The 2nd Canadian Division in particular found itself unable to seal off South Beveland. The German paratroopers of the 6th *Fallschirmjäger* Regiment, part of Battle Group Chill south and east of Bergen op Zoom, could not be dislodged from their positions. In an effort to force a breakthrough, the acting commander of the 1st Canadian Army (General Simonds) decided to push the 4th Canadian Armoured Division between the 49th British Division (Polar Bears) and the 2nd Canadian Division. To facilitate a smooth passage of lines, the 4th Canadian Armoured Division was temporarily placed under the command of the British I Corps. The objective of the operation, known as Operation "Suitcase," was to get behind the German lines at Woensdrecht and Bergen op Zoom and force the German paratroopers into a strategic retreat. Next, the access roads to Brabant from Tholen and St-Philipsland were to be secured and finally, the Germans were to be forced back across the Hollands Diep river to the north.

Operation Suitcase

Operation "Suitcase" was launched from Brasschaet, north of Antwerp (see Map I on p. 4). The advance of the 4th Canadian Armoured Division to Esschen was seriously hampered by mines, but no major engagements took place. After Esschen was secured, the small town of Wouwsche Plantage was the next target. Increasing resistance was met at this point and heavy fighting ensued before the Germans were eventually cleared from this area.

Following consolidation at Wouwsche Plantage, the 4th Canadian Division was divided into two brigade groups, to be commanded by the headquarters of the 4th Armoured Brigade and the 10th Infantry Brigade. The force commanded by the 4th Armoured Brigade moved north to Heerle, while the troops under the command of the 10th Infantry Brigade Group headed west to Huijbergen and Bergen op Zoom.

The success of the flanking manoeuvre east of Bergen op Zoom (the main road from Bergen op Zoom to Roosendaal was taken on 27 October) forced the German defenders to beat a hasty retreat. The town was liberated with a minimum of effort while the Germans hastily set up a new defensive position on the northern edge of Bergen op Zoom. The 10th Infantry Brigade attacked this position to clear the way to Steenbergen via Halsteren.

While Bergen Op Zoom was being liberated, the tanks of the 4th Armoured Brigade bypassed Heerle to the west and, with the exception of a few skirmishes, were able to reach Moerstraten without major difficulty. The Governor General's Foot Guards (GGFG), supported by "B" Coy of the Lake Superior Regiment (LSR), liberated Moerstraten on 29 October. A few skirmishes with the Germans took place on the outskirts of Moerstraten on the Steenbergen side and several tanks were put out of action. It quickly became obvious that the route via Oudlandsestraat (today Moerstraatseweg, MN13-16), which ran from Moerstraten (MN16) to Steenbergen, was well defended. Concerted action would be required to secure this main route from Bergen op Zoom to Steenbergen [4].

21 Army Group

First Canadian Army

2nd Canadian Army Artillery Group

59th British Artillery Group

II Canadian Corps

II Canadian Corps Artillery

2nd Canadian Armoured Brigade

I British Corps

2nd Canadian Infantry Division

POLAND

3rd Canadian Infantry Division

52nd Lowland Infantry Div.

MOUNTAIN

1st Polish Armoured Div.

4th Canadian Armoured Division

104 "Timberwolves" Infantry Div.

49 "Polar Bears" Infantry Div.

Badges of the Allied units involved in the Battle of the Scheldt (author's collection).

The German Fifteenth Army under General Gustav-Adolf von Zangen, having escaped the encirclement in Flanders by fleeing across the Scheldt, had orders to stop the Allied advance in the south-western region of the Netherlands. The now infamous Battle of Arnhem had driven a deep wedge into the German front, which meant that the city of 's-Hertogenbosch was under threat from both the south and the east, and the city of Eindhoven was deep in liberated territory. The 15th Army defended the area west of Nijmegen, while the 1st Paratrooper Army was positioned east of the Allied penetration.

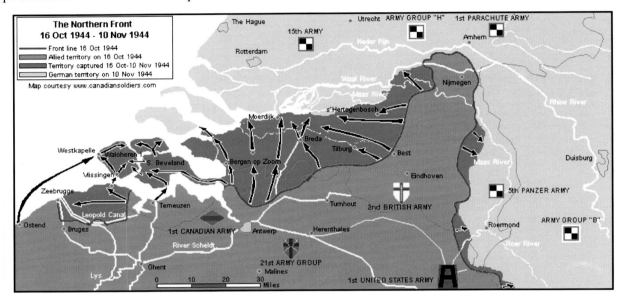

Map II: *The Northern Front, October/November 1944*

By mid-October, the divisions of the 15th Army occupied an area stretching from Zeeland Flanders / Walcheren to 's-Hertogenbosch region, with 88 Corps in the eastern sector and 67 Korps in the west. The 70th Division in Walcheren and the 64th Division in Western Zeeland Flanders were under the direct command of the 15th Army. It was the German 67 Corps, under the command of General Otto Sponheimer, that defended the Steenbergen sector with the so-called *Kampfgruppe Chill*. The 67 Corps included the 346th Division (sector Stampersgat - Standdaarbuiten), the 245th Division (sector Standdaarbuiten – Zevenbergschen-hoek), and the 711th Division (sector Zevenbergschenhoek - Raamsdonkveer) [2].

The Steenbergen region

Steenbergen is located in an ancient, wide-open polder landscape (the Kruisland polder was reclaimed in 1487), its soil an accretion of sea clay over a layer of peat. The polders are drained by innumerable ditches and canals, aided by pumping stations. The area, hemmed in by low dikes, is dotted with hamlets consisting of a handful of houses and crisscrossed by narrow roads lined with trees. Steenbergen received city rights in 1272, but since it was ravaged time and again by the wars that swept through the area, its oldest buildings date back to the 19th century,

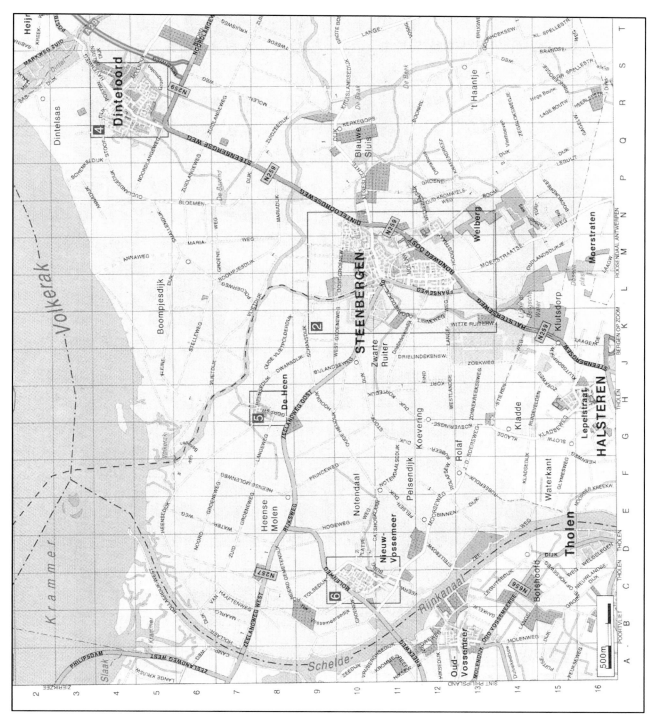

Map III: *Modern map of Steenbergen / Welberg and surroundings (© Falkplan BV)*

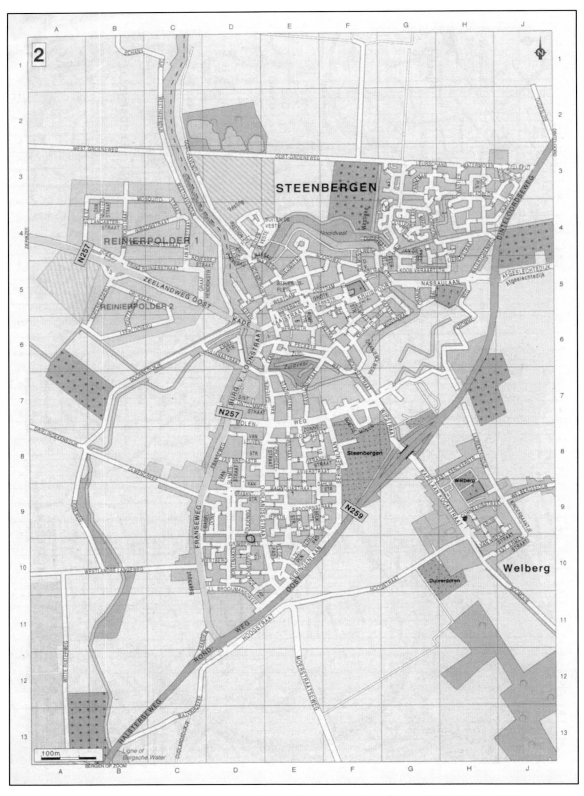

Map IV: *Modern map of Steenbergen and Welberg (© Falkplan BV)*

including the church with its 241 feet tall spire (the third tallest in the Netherlands). It was a fortified town, with its typical star-shaped form, surrounded by canals and dikes. The town itself currently has some 12,000 inhabitants. Welberg, located on a slight sandy rise, is a small community to the east of Steenbergen, today numbering around 1,500 inhabitants. In October/November 1944, much of the land was covered by four inches of water as a result of interference with and destruction of the pumping stations. This made the maze of ditches and canals difficult to spot under the layer of water and presented a formidable obstacle to an army on the move.

The line of defence around Steenbergen

The main German line of defence for the "Battle of Steenbergen" ran from the Eendracht canal at Glymesweg (F15) in the west via the hamlet of Kladde (G14) through the Westland along Koolbaantje (a street at the southern tip of Steenbergen) to Welberg along Hoogstraat (M12), and continued along the Welbergsedijk (NP12), via the hamlet of De Overval, to the Vliet, a river running roughly east to west north of Steenbergen. A general map of the German positions is given on page 16 (Map V).

On the western flank, the defence consisted of two strongpoints: the Glymes pumping station and the hamlet of Kladde. The defensive frontline in this region roughly followed the Scherminkel canal (no longer in existence). The two strongpoints were connected by a belt of road blocks and mine fields. This type of defence was deemed adequate since the polder country was completely unsuitable for tanks. As stated, the polders had been flooded and were covered in several centimetres of water, which made them even more inaccessible.

A number of earthen casemates, prepared in the fall of 1944 and reputedly equipped with the notorious 88 mm anti-aircraft guns, had been dug along Bergse Grintweg, the road that forms the western border of Steenbergen. Similar casemates had been dug in strategic positions from the Boomdijk (NQ12-16) to the Groenedijk (PQ12-16): at the Boomdijk past the hamlet of Bocht and at the end of Kinderbaantje, a street on the eastern edge of Welberg. The positions, camouflaged with nets, were completely invisible from a distance of a few hundred metres. The hamlet of Waterhoefke, just south of Steenbergen, was also a key defensive point, comparable to Kladde and the Glymes pumping station.

An uninterrupted, double row of barbed wire ran in a circular pattern around Steenbergen. The strip between the rows of barbed wire was studded with mines, and most intersections and waterway crossings in the "fortress" were also mined.

Further to the east of Welberg, the land was completely saturated with water, and the defensive measures were considerably less rigorous. The polder drainage canal to De Weel (a pond east of Steenbergen) was designated as an anti-tank ditch. This had been broadened and deepened in the fall of 1944 at the orders of the German occupiers. The line continued from De Weel to the Vliet river with another anti-tank ditch. The hamlet of Blauwe Sluis (Q10) formed an advance position to defend the eastern flank.

A belt of slit trenches ran through the woods along the Eekelendreef road (M13), and more had been dug in the orchard behind Corneliusstraat, which bisects Welberg from east to west, and behind the houses on Hoogstraat. This belt of slit trenches must have continued both eastward and westward. The houses along the Welbergsedijk road (NP12) had become part of the defence, with many occupied by Germans. A command centre of sorts was located in the basement of the Koolen family's farm house at the corner of the Boomdijk and Dwarsdijk roads (P13). The family itself had been evicted and was forced to live in a shelter dug into the dike. The house was declared off-limits to its residents.

Open farmland was strewn with so-called "Rommel Asparagus": bare wooden poles around two metres tall, set into the ground at regular intervals. Armenian soldiers serving in the German army had carried out much of this work during the summer and fall of 1944, but local residents had also been forced to work on the project. The purpose of the poles was to prevent, or at least hamper, glider landings. On most (polder) roads and dikes, every tree had been felled to be turned into Rommel Asparagus, and the denuded, flooded landscape around Steenbergen presented a bleak picture.

Anti-tank walls on all access roads

Both Oudlandse-straat (E12, Map IV) and the road across the Ligne river were blocked off by a concrete tank wall (see Map V, p. 16). The wall at the Ligne was open to traffic but could be sealed off by rolling a circular slab of concrete into position. The tank wall on Oudlandsestraat blocked the road completely, although the height of the wall on the road itself was less than in the adjoining area. An earthen access ramp led from the Steenbergen side o the Moerstraten side, where it became a wooden ramp. This ramp,

The remnants of the tank wall on Oudlandsestraat (now Moerstraatseweg) in the 1980's. This photo was taken looking towards Moerstraten (collection De Steenen Kamer *Historical Society).*

built some time prior to the Canadian attack, allowed traffic to pass through while the road could instantly be blocked by removing or dynamiting the wooden ramp. The ramp, however, disappeared on Crazy Tuesday[2] and the Germans constructed a single lane that bypassed the wall. It was mined at the approach of the Canadians.

---

[2] "Crazy Tuesday" refers to Tuesday September 5, 1944, when rumours spread that the liberation of the Netherlands was at hand. Dutch residents prepared to celebrate and to cheer on the Allied liberators. Many workers went home to wait for the Allies to arrive. German occupation forces and collaborators panicked and destroyed documents, and some fled back to Germany.

The Stoofdijk road (GJ10-11) towards Nieuw-Vossemeer, just outside the built-up area of Steenbergen, was also blocked by a wall, as were the Drielindekensdijk road (JL11-12) and Kruislanddijk road (RS10). Another tank wall was located on the Boomdijk road near the first Krabben bridge (P14), but it was never completed in the wake of "Crazy Tuesday" and did not play a part in the battle. The latter wall was of the same type as the one near the bridge across the Ligne but was not equipped with the circular concrete slab designed to close off the road [30].

Bridges and culverts blown up

The bridges and culverts along the access roads to Welberg and Steenbergen were blown up before the arrival of the Canadian attackers. At the Westlandse Langeweg bridge across the Ligne river (K12), the explosion caused a hole in the pavement, but it was possible to cross the bridge on foot skirting the hole on either side. The Witte Ruijter bridge across the Ligne (K14), further to the south, was also blown up but could be crossed on foot. The bridge at Blauwe Sluis (Q10) was destroyed as well, as was the bridge over the Breede Watergang (P10) and the Vliet. The culvert on Oudlandsestraat over the Oudlandse Watergang was completely destroyed, as was the bridge across the Boomvaart (P15) near the hamlet of Bocht. The first Krabben bridge or "Padmoes bridge" (P14) rested in the water at a crazy angle and the bridge across the drainage canal near the Groenedijk had also been destroyed. An attempt to blow up the junction of the Oudlandse Watergang and the Boomvaart (P14) had been largely unsuccessful.

German units in the Battle of Steenbergen

The German defence positions were manned by three units, supplemented by the remnants of an Assault Gun Brigade (the 667th *Panzerjagdabteilung*). The soldiers of the Third Battalion, 6th *Fallschirmjäger* (Paratroop) Regiment were positioned on the western flank (west of the tank wall on Oudlandsestraat). Troops of 10 Coy of that unit had adopted positions near

When this German self-propelled assault gun ran out of fuel, its crew drove it into the Boomvaart, near the corner of Krommeweg and Molenweg (J5, Map IV) (coll. P. Adriaansen).

13

Waterhoefke. Lieutenant Colonel Dreyer assumed command of the 6th *Fallschirmjäger* Regiment on 27 October. At the time of writing, the exact location of his command centre was not known, but it was likely nearby or in Dinteloord. The Hermann Goering *Ersatz- und Ausbildungs-Regiment* (reserve and training regiment) was positioned in Welberg and the woods, and troops from the 1st Battalion, 937th Grenadier Regiment of the 245th Infantry Division, were also present.

The newly arrived German soldiers were of a different calibre from those who had been stationed in Steenbergen during the occupation. They were identifiable by their clothing: the Hermann Goering troops wore light-yellow uniforms instead of the field grey of the occupation troops. Local residents generally viewed the newcomers as callous and indifferent, referring to them as a "rough bunch." The father of Kees van Eekelen of the Witkruis farm in Welberg had his watch confiscated without so much as a by-your-leave, accompanied by a flood of curses ("Scheisse") and orders to shut his trap ("Halt's Maul!"). A number of sources confirm that these German soldiers were often dead drunk during the battles.

The self-propelled assault gun from the Boomvaart was moved to the market square at a later date. Two heavy trucks were required to hoist this steel colossus from the canal (collection P. Adriaansen).

Finally, at least six self-propelled assault guns[3] (*Sturmgeschütze*) were positioned a short distance behind the German line. Canadian sources mention the presence of a Tiger tank. The exact number and type of armoured vehicles was not known at the time of writing. What is known is that at least one German SPG patrolled up and down Molenweg (M11) and was

---

[3] The acronym "SPG' will be used in the remainder of this book to refer to self-propelled (assault) guns.

eventually abandoned in the Boomvaart canal. After the liberation, this vehicle was put on display in Steenbergen's market square. Two more of these vehicles patrolled the Maria dike for a day or two, along the northern bank of the Vliet river. The exact dates are not known.

The orders of the German defenders

The German objective was to delay the Canadian advance in order to allow the remainder of their troops (approximately 1,500 men) to retreat to Numansdorp via Dintelsas and Willemstad. It was never their intention to put a definite halt to the Allied advance at Steenbergen and it is estimated that the Germans defending Steenbergen numbered no more than 600 [34].

Map V. *Canadian ordnance map showing the German defence line around Steenbergen. The map, produced on 17 October 1944 based on aerial reconnaissance, was marked up with the German positions. The artillery positions shown below, based on verbal accounts, generally correspond to the artillery positions mentioned in Canadian combat reports.*

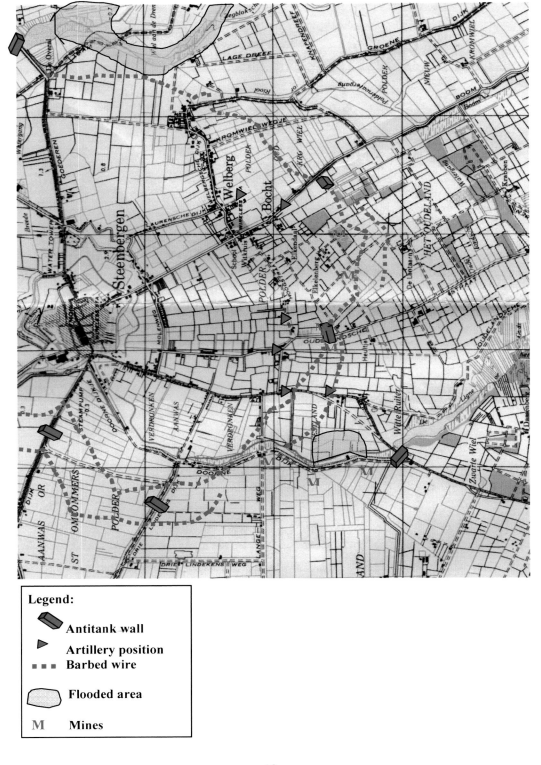

Legend:

▱ Antitank wall

▶ Artillery position

▪▪▪ Barbed wire

◯ Flooded area

M Mines

Sunday 29 October, the day the Governor General's Foot Guards liberated Moerstraten, was a cool, dry day.

The Foot Guards cross the Halsters Laag

In order to cut off the Germans retreating from the river Zoom, the Foot Guards had orders to reach the main road between Steenbergen and Halsteren to the south. It was important to physically seal off the main road to block German troop movements and hopefully cut off a substantial number of enemies in the vicinity of Halsteren. Unfortunately, this could not be accomplished by using direct fire nor could the effectiveness of indirect fire be determined.

The commander of the Foot Guards, Lieutenant Colonel Smith, issued orders to advance in a westerly direction from Moerstraten towards the main road from Halsteren to Steenbergen (see Map VI, p. 20). Given that the terrain between Moerstraten and Halsteren was quite unsuitable for tanks, this was a very risky decision.

It should be noted that tank crews are virtually blind in the dark. The field of vision of a tank driver is restricted to what he can see through a 15 cm by 3 cm periscope that quickly becomes useless when it becomes covered in spattered mud. Once that happens, the commander must raise his head and upper body out of the turret and give the driver instructions through the intercom.

No. 3 Squadron, led by Major Lewis, entered the Halsters Laag from the direction of Moerstraten with eight tanks (the Halsters Lowlands [map III, K15] was a swampy area left behind by an ancient, former sea arm). They split up into two groups: three tanks under the command of Lieutenant Finlayson and four tanks commanded by Lieutenant McKergon. The Major followed in his own tank. The motorized infantry of "B" Coy, Lake Superior Regiment, accompanied the tanks. Each group was forced to halt when one of its tanks bogged down in the mud, but the vehicles were recovered by sheer force of effort and the journey was resumed.

Along the way, the tanks fired on a large number of farm houses and left them in flames. They encountered little or no resistance from the Germans and it is believed that the tank crews, virtually blind, employed speculative fire on every building they encountered as a precautionary measure.[4]

The mud made it impossible to continue cross-country, forcing the crews to follow the roads. This put them further to the south than was desirable and they emerged at the Bergsewater (or Ligne) river in line with Klutsdorp (K16). The infantrymen of the Lake Superior Regiment had great difficulty digging in because the groundwater level was only a few centimetres below the surface. A miserably cold and wet night ensued.

---

[4] Several written [22] and oral sources mention Germans setting fire to farm houses in the Halsters Lowlands. Based on the sources consulted, the author is of the opinion that no Germans were present in the area during the Foot Guards' advance. The regimental history [14] makes no direct mention of deliberate firing on farm houses and leaving them in flames, but it does refer to firing at targets where "Germans might conceivably be present."

While No. 3 Squadron opened fire in the direction of Oudemolen (south of Klutsdorp) and De Handwijzer (a café) at the intersection of the road to Lepelstraat and the main road from Steenbergen to Bergen op Zoom (J16), the rest of the regiment was able to catch up with the tanks that had driven ahead. The route was marked by burning farm houses. En route, No. 2 Squadron's front tank bogged down at a bend in the road. Major Baylay, the squadron's commander, dismounted and reconnoitred on foot but was unable to find a suitable bypass. Colonel Smith stepped in and ordered the Regiment (less No. 3 Squadron, which was already in position at the Bergsewater river) to proceed straight across the fields in the direction of the Bergsewater. As expected, a number of tanks bogged down in the mud. The crew of the armoured recovery vehicle (ARV) was kept fully occupied that night pulling stranded tanks out of the mud. Despite all the setbacks, the regiment managed to regroup with No. 3 Squadron by early morning. Brigadier Moncel at brigade headquarters received the news that the Foot Guards had reached the Bergsewater with disbelief [14].

An "orders group" of the Foot Guards' staff, late October 1944. From left to right: Major G.T. Baylay, Lt.-Col. E.M. Smith, Majors M.M. Morell and J.K. Hjalmarson, Captain G.M. Alexander, and Major G.C. Lewis (PA138445).

Given the circumstances and the terrain, the advance of the Foot Guards through the Halsters Lowlands was truly an extraordinary achievement. Canadian tank tactics did not provide for deploying tanks in the dark due to the limitations mentioned above. Virtually blind and at night, the Foot Guard tanks were an easy target for an enemy equipped with anti-tank weapons.

The appendix in the back of this publication presents several citations for bravery decorations awarded in connection with the action described above.

The Germans retreat to Steenbergen

Despite the fact that the trap had snapped shut thanks to the impressive achievement of the Foot Guards, the end result was disappointing. The Germans managed to escape just in time, moving towards Steenbergen. At around 1600 hrs on 29 October, a patrol of the GGFG operating in a far-forward position reported still seeing German military traffic on the main road. After that, there was no sign of any Germans.

As early as 29 October, the German high command issued orders that, due to the Allied breakthrough north of Heerle, the troops should fall back to the Nieuw-Vossemeer – Steenbergen line, since the available forces were insufficient to offer effective resistance. General von Zangen, commander of the 15th Army, provided the following information in a message to 88 Corps stationed near 's-Hertogenbosch [37]:

[...] *5) Raum 67 A.K. setzt sich nachts 29. / 30. 10 mit Masse auf Linie NIEUW VOSSEMER – VOORM FORT HENDRIK – STEENBERGSCHE VLIET – STAMPERSGAT - DINTEL – MARK – KANAL - OOSTERHOUT ab. Die zu verteidigen ist. STEENBERGEN als vorgeschobenen Stuetzpunkt halten.* [...]

[...] 5) 67th Army Corps operational area: move to the Nieuw-Vossemeer – former Fort Hendrik – Steenbergse Vliet - Stampersgat – Dintel – Markkanaal – Oosterhout line during the night of 29/30 October. To be defended. Retain Steenbergen as advance strongpoint. [...]

The German positions on the north bank of the river Zoom were abandoned as ordered and the 10th Canadian Brigade made contact with the tanks of the Foot Guards on 30 October shortly after they arrived at the main road. Following the German retreat, there was no further contact with the enemy, and Halsteren was liberated without a shot fired.

In the hamlet of Lepelstraat, the last German guns had moved out at around 2100 hrs on 28 October, departing in a northerly direction. At approximately 0550 hrs on Sunday 29 October, the German military engineers who had stayed behind blew up the bell tower [22].

Meanwhile, among the population of Welberg and Steenbergen

Ad Helmons lived on a street called Koolbaantje. This street, which disappeared after the war during the construction of the ring road around Steenbergen, was situated at the southern tip of Steenbergen, approximately where Brooijmansdreef is today (D10, Map IV). Ad's location on Koolbaantje gave him a good vantage point to observe the retreating Germans:

The Germans moved along Koolbaantje in tanks and all sorts of vehicles, coming from the direction of Halsteren. All during the night of 29 to 30 October, you could hear and smell the presence of large groups of Germans. The soldiers' leather outfits gave off a peculiar smell of leather mixed with sour sweat. The positions that had been dug around Steenbergen in the fall were manned. They were so well camouflaged that they were completely invisible. The assault guns had been covered with branches and when they were stationary, they were difficult to spot. In the fields behind the houses on Koolbaantje, six SPGs sat firing in a line abreast. The vehicles were moved after every salvo to avoid Canadian counter-fire. [verbal account, Ad Helmons]

The inhabitants of Welberg received warning of the coming attack from an unknown bicyclist who managed to spread the news by ringing his bell. The incident is mentioned in a municipal report produced after the liberation. In all probability, the bicyclist was dispatched by the Germans. The inhabitants were ordered to stay off the streets after five o'clock and to keep their windows and doors shut. According to one oral source, it was a German truck mounted with speakers that passed the word, rather than a bicyclist. The truck reportedly drove along the Welbergsedijk road, disseminating a similar message.

Urged on by the Germans, many Welberg families fled to Nieuw-Vossemeer, De Heen, or Notendaal. Those who remained behind descended into their shelters or moved to Steenbergen, where a sugar factory offered shelter. The Charitas hospital on Kleine Kerkstraat took in some 2,000 people. When the hospital was full, people were sent on to the storage sheds near the Havendijk, where many found refuge. The sheds offered no facilities whatsoever, with the exception of a supply of burlap bags that could be used as blankets. That night, the first shells hit Steenbergen [21].

The Battle of Steenbergen begins...

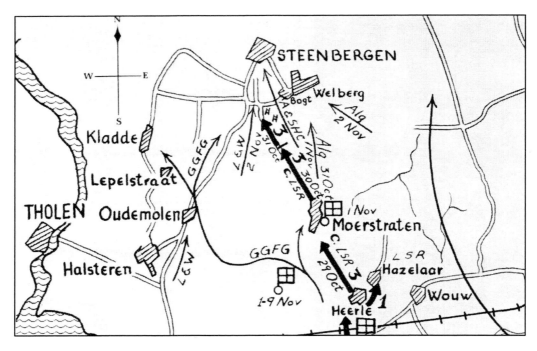

Map VI. *A fragment of a map from the regimental history of the Canadian Grenadier Guards. It gives a diagram of the advance of the units of the 4th Armoured Brigade. The bold numeral 3 above Heerle refers to No. 3 Squadron of the Canadian Grenadier Guards [15].*

Monday 30 October was dry and cold. All day, the sun remained hidden behind a thick layer of clouds. A few rain showers fell in the evening and during the night.

The situation as observed from Koolbaantje

Around noon on Monday, 30 October, the tank wall on the bridge over the Ligne was locked down. As mentioned, the wall was equipped with a circular slab of concrete that could be rolled across the opening. Two more SPGs crossed the bridge at the last minute, moving towards the Moerstraten front via Oudlandsestraat.

The final traffic in the direction of Steenbergen consisted of a few ambulances and trucks. They cautiously navigated past the mud along the tank wall on Oudlandsestraat and sped off towards Steenbergen. When the last vehicle had cleared the wall, the track bypassing the wall was mined. By 1600 hrs, all activity had ceased. The German troops had evidently all been pulled back behind the new defensive line around Steenbergen.

A short time later, the Governors General's Foot Guards could be heard across the Ligne river. At the sound of machine gun fire from Waterhoefke towards Oudlandsestraat, the families living along Koolbaantje hastily made for their shelters.

Sector Oudlandsestraat

On 29 October, the tanks of the Foot Guards in Moerstraten were relieved by No. 3 Squadron[5] of the Canadian Grenadier Guards, led by Major Hale, with "C" Coy, Lake Superior Regiment, under command. On 30 October at 0915 hrs, the Lake Superior Regiment moved off towards Steenbergen via Oudlandsestraat, followed at a distance by the tanks of No. 3 Squadron CGG. Brigade headquarters ordered them to advance to Steenbergen at all possible speed. According to the information available at headquarters, the enemy had already left.

The culvert across the Krabben canal was reached at 1345 hrs and although it had been blown up, crossing the canal did not prove to be a major obstacle. At 1405 hrs, the group reached the Oudlandse Watergang canal. The destruction of the bridge at this location did present a problem, since the gap to be crossed measured nearly seven metres. Assault boats were requisitioned post-haste to ferry the infantry across the water. Supported by the tanks, the men of "C" Coy, Lake Superior Regiment, crossed the drainage canal in two boats at 0105 hrs (31 October). The attackers immediately came under heavy machine gun fire. After ten minutes, the situation started to improve. Keeping the bridgehead under mortar fire, the Germans moved off towards the north, to the defensive belt surrounding Steenbergen [15].

---

[5] As a point of interest, although the Governor General's Foot Guards and the Canadian Grenadier Guards converted to an armoured role in 1942, they continued to use numbers in referring to their squadrons, contrary to the usual practice in armoured regiments of using letters. Thus, "No. 1 Squadron" in the GGFG and the CGG would be known as "A" squadron in the other armoured regiments. See p. 103.

The engineers from 3 Troop of 9 Field Squadron (under command of 8 Field Squadron) filled an enormous crater that day in the pavement on Oudlandsestraat, just outside Moerstraten. This hole was likely caused when the culvert across the Krabben was blown up [16].

On the Peeters' farm

A minor drama unfolded at the Peeters' farm, target of the attack by the Lake Superior Regiment. In a drunken stupor, some of the German occupiers threatened to set the farm house on fire. The family in the cellar tried to leave, together with a family from Tholen with whom they shared the house, but the Germans blocked the exit to ensure that the occupants perished in the already burning house. The panicked occupants fled through another exit and jumped into a water-filled ditch. One of them, a girl, could not keep up with the group and took shelter behind a millstone as bullets whizzed through the air. Her mother, convinced that her daughter had been killed, went berserk and tried to drown herself in the ditch. One of the men managed to keep the woman's head above water and the girl was able to rejoin the group shortly afterwards. Meanwhile, the Canadians had arrived. A Canadian officer yelled at the civilians to get away and head for Moerstraten because more fighting was expected. One member of the group stayed long enough to watch the Canadians fire the anti-tank weapons (*Panzerfausts*) left behind by the Germans. Then he ran off to catch up with the others, heading for a safer location via the ditch.

In the shelters on Koolbaantje

That evening, the Germans evicted the Nijssen family from their shelter and requisitioned it for their own use. The Nijssens had no choice but to join other residents in their shelter down the street. Two very frightened Germans furtively crept into the house of the De Jong family, timidly asking for shelter and civilian clothing. Mr de Jong correctly judged that this would expose them to great danger and told the men to leave. The next day, as the De Jongs fled to Notendaal, they saw one of the two men lying dead beside the road.

Soon after that, the first shells exploded over Koolbaantje with a thundering crash. The war erupted in all its intensity, accompanied by ear-shattering noise. The difference between the machine guns of friend and foe was clearly discernible. The German machine guns had an extremely high rate of fire and sounded like the ripping of cloth, while the Canadian Bren gun was identifiable by its dry cracks, coming at a slower rate.

The airless shelters shook and heaved under the impacts; dust and soil rained down on the frightened occupants. The air, saturated with gun smoke and dust kicked up by the shells, was difficult to breathe. The concussion waves generated by the exploding shells were hardest to bear. People's breath caught in their throats and they felt as if their ear drums were bursting. The women clasped their rosaries and never stopped praying. The men masked their fear by cursing and swearing.

The entrance to one of the shelters faced in the direction of Moerstraten, allowing its occupants to watch the battle for the bridgehead over the Oudlandse Watergang in the dark. Red dots of tracer fire raced across the sky in crisscross patterns. Dozens of artillery shells smacked into the pavement with a metallic clang, bouncing off in all directions. In different circumstances, it would have been a spectacular fireworks display.

Late that night, the people on Koolbaantje once again heard groups of Germans in the street, passing along the Oudlandsedijk road and headed in the direction of Oudlandsestraat. These were no doubt defenders being pulled back in preparation for the attack by the Lake Superior Regiment across the Oudlandse Waterweg. They adopted prepared defensive positions near the tank wall.

Some time during that night, a blackened face suddenly appeared in the opening of the shelter occupied by the Helmons family. Frightened, they stared up into the face of a taciturn soldier, the white of his eyes accentuated by the camouflage paint. To their profound relief, the soldier proved to be a Canadian, a member of a reconnaissance patrol of between six to ten soldiers (probably from the Lake Superior Regiment, positioned near De Handwijzer –J16). They were wearing sneakers to allow them to make their way past the German lines unheard. A moment later, they melted back into the night.

Soon after that, a German officer appeared and shone a flashlight down into the shelter. The occupants were paralyzed with fear. Silently, he counted the number of people present. The same officer returned several times that night and in the days that followed, to count the number of occupants. In all likelihood, he was looking for deserters dressed in civilian clothing.

In the thick of the artillery barrage, a member of the Helmons family suddenly decided he needed to inspect the house, which had already received five hits. The devastation was immense and he found himself forced to take shelter there. Some time later, two drunken Germans stumbled into the house, looking for food. Trembling, he pointed to a pan of sour soup and fled back to the shelter. Fortunately, the hungry soldiers overlooked the slaughtered pig in the cellar below the house, which would be a godsend for the Helmons later on.

Sector Lepelstraat, Glymes, Kladde

As mentioned, the GGFG had halted at the Bergsewater river, which they had reached via the Halsters Lowlands. They dispatched patrols towards both Klutsdorp and Oudemolen to assess the chances of reaching the main road. The northern route was out of the question because of the woods and the condition of the ground, which was saturated with water. Meanwhile, Oudemolen and De Handwijzer came under renewed fire at 0800 hrs.

At around 1000 hrs, the Foot Guards continued their advance based on information gathered by one of the patrols, which had discovered a feasible route in the direction of Oudemolen (south of Klutsdorp). No. 1 Squadron, under Major Alexander, reported at 1116 hrs that the enemy had abandoned Oudemolen. By noon, they made contact with the 10th Infantry Brigade, which had moved northwards from the river Zoom. The trap had now snapped shut. The Foot Guards and the infantrymen of "B" Coy, Lake Superior Regiment, regrouped near Oudemolen.

That same morning, a section of No. 1 Squadron went out on patrol to Klutsdorp (K16), where they destroyed a German machine gun nest in a brief skirmish, roughly 100 metres northeast of the main road. Another section was sent towards Kladde (H15) at around 1535 hrs. When they arrived in Lepelstraat (G16), they found that they were the first liberators to be encountered by the local population. The men and the tanks received an enthusiastic welcome and cigarettes were exchanged for a few drinks. When the Canadians inquired about the whereabouts of the Germans, people pointed in the direction of the German positions near the

Glymes pumping station and Kladde. A patrol of five or six tanks led by Sergeant Kimberly encountered a very active enemy. From the Kladde resistance pocket, the German defenders blew up the crossing over the canal right in front of the Canadian tanks. Skirting Kladde on the west side also proved impossible. Anti-tank fire and mines caused the patrol to beat a hasty retreat at around 1720 hrs [14].

The Canadian 23rd Field Regiment (SP) reported on 30 October that it was taking up positions in Halsteren at approximately 1600 hrs in order to direct harassing fire at the western sector (Lepelstraat, Glymes, Kladde) [11].

That night, the Germans evicted the inhabitants of Kladde and sent them off to Nieuw-Vossemeer (D11). The same fate befell the refugees on the farm of the Vriens family, since the farm had become part of the reinforced German position at the end of Glymesweg (F16) [22].

The polder region west of Halsteren was sparsely occupied by the British Columbia Regiment and "A" Squadron, 12th Manitoba Dragoons, while the main force of the Canadians was positioned along the Halsterseweg road and near Moerstraten. With the Germans in position at the Glymes pumping station and near Kladde, and the Canadians positioned near Klutsdorp/ Lepelstraat, the area extending west into the polder turned into a sort of no-man's land. The village of Lepelstraat was sporadically hit by shells from both the German and Canadian lines. This unfortunate situation deprived the residents of even the barest necessities of life. It was impossible to evacuate their injured and they had no medical facilities whatsoever. One or two people managed to make their way to Halsteren via a small back road to get help, food, and information for the families left behind. The situation in Lepelstraat did not improve until the 2nd of November, when infantrymen of the 8th Light Anti-Aircraft Regiment would take up position in Lepelstraat [18].

Sector Witte Ruiter

Early in the afternoon, the commanding officer of the Governor General's Foot Guards, Lieutenant Colonel Smith, ordered No. 1 Squadron (Captain Alexander) to advance to Steenbergen via the Halsterseweg road. Together with "B" Coy, Lake Superior Regiment, the tanks set out with Lieutenant Venus's troop in the lead. The advance proceeded without incident as far as the partially destroyed bridge over the Ligne (K13), which they reached at around 1600 hrs. German mortar fire caused casualties among the accompanying infantry. The road was relatively narrow, so that the tanks were unable to manoeuvre freely. They were further restricted by the tall trees that lined the road and prevented the tank gun barrels from traversing. Just before the bridge and on towards Steenbergen, the landscape became wide open, which was a decided advantage for an enemy equipped with anti-tank guns. The infantry nevertheless crossed the Ligne river to establish a bridgehead, which caused the harassing fire of the German mortars to intensify. Since only the two front tanks were able to lay down suppressive fire, it was impossible to provide effective fire support. Some of the tanks in the rear of the column attempted to advance along the verge but soon ran into mines, which put two tanks out of action. The disabled tanks of Sergeant Prophet and Corporal Gordon made it impossible for the others to reverse and escape that way, and this provided the Germans with an excellent opportunity to strike. Anti-tank shells knocked out the front and rear tanks. The massive 88 mm armour-piercing shells penetrated the hulls of the Sherman tanks like a hot knife through butter. Sergeant

Ketcheson, one of the two commanders of the destroyed tanks, was injured and would eventually lose an eye. Lieutenant Canavan, the other tank commander, was lucky enough to escape unharmed. Guardsman Gardipee was killed, and Guardsmen Lavson, Westman, and Wheeler were injured. The scene was one of utter chaos. In addition to the anti-tank fire, the German also kept up their mortar bombardment. An armoured vehicle carrying a number of injured men and crews from damaged tanks attempted to escape along the verge but it, too, hit a mine and was put out of action.

In the course of the day, several sections of the 8th Field Squadron of the Canadian Engineers were sent towards Halsteren to build a Bailey bridge across the Ligne river "if circumstances permitted." Lieutenant Zimmerman was put in charge of the bridge builders. They arrived in Oudemolen from Halsteren with all the components and tools required to build a twenty-metre long bridge. Lieutenant Zimmerman conducted a reconnaissance of the bridgehead across the Ligne and found that the Lake Superior Regiment infantry were dug in at a distance of no more than fifty metres from the river. The situation at the bridgehead was so unstable that it was impossible to attempt construction that day [40].

Disabled Sherman tank somewhere in Steenbergen. This photo was probably taken on Bergse Grintweg, since that was the only road with a concrete pavement. (collection P. Adriaansen).

The infantry eventually managed to clear the mines, allowing the disorganised column of Foot Guards tanks to retreat some four hundred metres to Klutsdorp. The enemy fire came to a sudden halt.

The men relaxed and dismounted from their vehicles, but it turned out to be a trap: an hour later, their position came under renewed artillery fire. Fortunately, this trick injured only one man: Lance-Corporal McKillop. They were ordered to pull their tanks back to Oudemolen and by 1930 hrs, they were back in the position they had occupied that morning.

The infantrymen of the Lake Superior Regiment, however, were still dug in on the opposite side of the Ligne river and were taking heavy fire. The German anti-tank guns were especially active. In the cacophony of battle noise, the frightened soldiers heard the sound of German vehicles gathering unseen in front of their hastily dug positions. Meanwhile, the German heavy artillery zeroed in on the position and opened fire. At 2022 hrs, the headquarters of the Lake Superior Regiment decided to evacuate the bridgehead. The relatively small group of Canadians would not be able to hold out against a German assault, especially if this was supported by tanks. Under the cover of heavy shelling by the

The Germans blew up the water tower of Steenbergen. This photo shows the sad result (collection P. Adriaansen).

Canadian artillery, the LSR retreated across the Ligne and took up position near Klutsdorp. Planning im-mediately got underway for a second attempt on the following day.

That night, No. 3 Squadron led by Lieutenant Fritz was sent forward from Oudemolen to locate the German anti-tank guns. The squadron functioned as bait by firing in the direction of Steenbergen and Kladde and then changing position, repeating this action a number of times. This made it possible to pinpoint the German anti-tank guns that were returning fire, based on flash spotting and sound ranging.

The infantrymen of the Lake Superior Regiment also conducted a patrol. This was probably the same patrol that was in contact with the people in the Koolbaantje shelter, as mentioned earlier. The reconnaissance patrol did not encounter any enemies that night [14].

The first victim in Welberg

Close-up of the destruction of the water tower of Steenbergen (collection P. Adriaansen)

In Welberg, the war claimed its first civilian victim that day. Oral sources report that there was no major artillery bombardment but that shells fell at irregular intervals and in an irregular pattern. Most likely, the entire region had become the target of harassing fire. Cornelius Smout, age 35, was hit in the neck by a shell fragment. He died while working on the shelter behind his small house on Hoogstraat.

The destruction of the Gummarus church tower

In Steenbergen, the Germans prepared to blow up the bell tower of the Gummarus church, forcing residents to carry some 1500 kilograms of dynamite up to the tower. The town crier informed the residents of the impending explosion.

Father Uijtdewilligen, the curate, notified the resistance in Steenbergen, and Roel van Kaam, Koos Veraart, and the Van Mechelen brothers tried to sabotage the detonation. They presented themselves as clockmakers, sent to save the clock. Regrettably, they were kept under constant observation and did not have an opportunity to cut the wires. All the same, the first attempt by the Germans to blow up the tower failed. The explosives were finally detonated by shells fired from an SPG parked on Blauwstraat (G4, Map IV). The bell tower collapsed at 1800 hrs, following a huge explosion that shattered every window in the vicinity.

The collapse of the tower caused severe damage to the roof of the church. Fortunately, the German plan to blow up the tower had been in place for some time and the residents of Steenbergen had advance knowledge. This gave them the opportunity to remove the pews, statues, and other items from the interior of the church shortly before the tower was blown up.

The Gummarus church after the liberation. The church was not completely restored until many years later (collection P. Adriaansen).

Around the same time, vessels were sunk in Steenbergen's harbour and explosive charges were placed in the water tower and under several bridges in the vicinity [21]. In Welberg, the bridge across the Boomvaart near the hamlet of Bocht was blown up. The following day, the water tower and all the other structures that had been mined were also blown up.

Destroying tall buildings before a retreat was routine procedure, intended to deny the enemy vantage points, but it is not clear why the Germans chose to blow up the bell tower at that particular moment. The Canadians were nowhere near the town at the time, nor was the German defence in peril of collapsing. In fact, the tower could have been useful to the Germans as an observation post had they elected to leave it standing.

The British exchange fire with the Germans near Blauwe Sluis (Q10)

As previously mentioned, the British 49th "Polar Bear" Infantry Division advanced on the right flank of the Canadian 4th Armoured Division. By the 31st of October, they had reached the hamlet of Kruisland (east of Steenbergen). At around 1515 hrs, a patrol of the reconnaissance regiment of this division set out for the Kruislandsedijk road (RS10) via Langeweg (T10-11). At the intersection of these two roads, the patrol came under German fire from the hamlet of

Blauwe Sluis. According to the patrol report, the fire was accurately aimed and heavy. The patrol concluded that the defence at Blauwe Sluis was vigorous indeed.

The Germans also destroyed the church of Kruisland (collection P. Adriaansen).

There is no information suggesting that additional attempts were made to reach Steenbergen along this right flank. Presumably, the corps commander ordered the 49th Division to push north to Stampersgat (on the Vliet river) instead of making a detour to the west, since the overall purpose of the operation was to encircle the Germans at Willemstad and the Moerdijk bridge. In addition, an advance by the 49th Division would cross divisional borders, which would considerably increase the risk of casualties from friendly fire [36].

Tuesday 31 October was a dry day in spite of a heavy overcast. The temperature remained cool throughout the day.

Sector Oudlandsestraat

As mentioned earlier, the Oudlandsestraat bridge over the canal had been blown up and the infantrymen of the Lake Superior Regiment crossed the Oudlandse Watergang in assault boats. At around 0145, Canadian engineers arrived at the shattered culvert. Lieutenant Lake (8th Field Squadron) had orders to erect a 50' DS Bailey bridge[6] across the drainage canal to enable the tanks to cross, since they were urgently needed to reinforce the bridgehead. By 0345 hrs, the infantry at the bridgehead had dug in positions approximately 400 metres from the canal and near the farm owned by the Peeters family. As soon as it became light and the ground fog cleared, the Germans opened fire on the position at the bridge, seriously hampering the construction work. Only the foundation of the Bailey Bridge had been completed by first light and to make matters worse, the assembly of the bridge components suffered a series of setbacks. In addition to the hindrance of the mortar fire, a bulldozer bogged down in the mud and a heavy truck carrying bridge components drove into the ditch bordering the road and became stuck. The shelling increased in intensity and eventually the situation became so dangerous that activities had to be suspended. Two engineers were injured during this attempt.

Major Edward "Ned" Amy was awarded the Distinguished Service Order for his actions at the bridgehead across the Oudlandse Watergang [15].

No. 3 Squadron, Canadian Grenadier Guards, had meanwhile been replaced by No. 1 Squadron led by Major Ned Amy. One of the troops under Major Amy's command (3 Troop, Lieutenant Muir) supported the bridge builders with direct fire from their tanks. Lieutenant Muir spread out his tanks on the Moerstraten side of the canal, so that each tank provided support to a platoon of the Lake Superior Regiment on the opposite side. As mentioned, German mortar fire started at dawn, hampering the engineers' efforts to erect the bridge. The Germans also unexpectedly attacked the bridgehead with soldiers armed with *panzerfausts* and supported by an SPG. The bridgehead of the Lake Superior Regiment was under serious pressure. Lieutenant Muir crossed on foot to improve the aim of the tanks by direct observation. Fortunately, the Canadian defenders of the bridgehead managed to repel the attack [15].

Since it was clear that the advance could not continue without a bridge over the Oudlandse Waterweg, it was decided to complete the bridge in spite of the hazardous situation. Major Allen (the commander of 8th Field Squadron) asked for volunteers among the engineers to complete the work. He apparently felt that giving the men a direct order to go to work under these circumstances could not be morally justified. The tanks of the Canadian Grenadier

---

[6] See Appendix I for a brief explanation of Bailey Bridges.

Guards again supported the construction of the bridge by laying down harassing fire. Eventually, the aim of the German guns grew less accurate, and the bridge was finished at 1017 hrs. The bank on the Welberg side of the crossing alone yielded 18 anti-tank mines. At 1025 hrs, the engineers waved to signal that the bridge was ready, and Major Amy crossed the Bailey bridge to stabilize the situation at the small bridgehead [16, 40].

One of the waiting tanks was manned by Hank Maiden and his crew. In his memoirs, Neil Stewart, who served with the Grenadier Guards, quotes the men who were watching the construction of the bridge:

Look at those guys out there. Mortar shells raining down there, and they work in it anyhow," said Hank. "Then they give us a big wave and run back off the bridge to let us go ahead, as if we're the brave ones going on ahead. Meanwhile they go back to the delightful task of lifting mines somewhere, just to keep their interest up. If they don't get killed up there building a bridge for us, they risk getting their heads blown off by an exploding mine. Those guys have more nerve than anyone else around, and get less credit for it too. [47]

Uniform of Private McCullough, Lake Superior Regiment (author's collection).

Uniform of an unidentified sergeant of the Canadian Grenadier Guards (author's collection).

Major Amy's group consisted of a troop of Stuart reconnaissance tanks and several Sherman tanks. The plan was to advance to Steenbergen, followed by three platoons of the Lake Superior Regiment, led by Major Dawson.

When the tanks arrived at the bridgehead, a three-tank patrol was sent off towards Welberg. Two reconnaissance tanks were put out of action by mines at 1140 hrs, near the entrance to the Panhoef farm. The rest of the assault group that had remained behind spread out along the road, but the multitude of mines and the accurate German harassing fire that followed made it impossible to continue the advance. Lieutenant Frederick Morrison, Guardsman Brock Bendal, Sergeant John Martin, and Lance Sergeant John Kearney were killed during this action. Guardsmen Walker and Walton were wounded. They were all members of the Canadian Grenadier Guards.

A short time later, around 1600 hrs, an infantry patrol was sent out to reconnoitre the situation at the intersection of Hoogstraat and Oudlandsestraat (E11, Map IV). They reported the presence of the tank wall, but attempts to clear the route of mines were unsuccessful. The German harassing fire, particularly from the direction of the hamlet of Bocht, made the situation too dangerous.

In the evening, at approximately 2130 hrs, the Algonquins who had been dispatched from Bergen op Zoom passed Major Amy's troops on the small bridgehead to conduct a night attack on Welberg and the tank wall. The Algonquin Regiment was temporarily attached to the 4th Armoured Brigade for this attack. The Canadian Grenadier Guards and the Lake Superior Regiment maintained their positions that night and defended the bridgehead over the Oudlandse Waterweg [15].

Night attack on Welberg

The warning order for a night attack on Steenbergen went out over the radio net to the staff of the 4th Armoured Brigade from division commander Major General Harry Foster at approximately 1200 hrs. By 1305 hrs, orders had been issued. The general stated that in his opinion, the advance was losing momentum. If the advance of the Foot Guards and the Grenadier Guards did not produce more positive results, the Algonquin Regiment would have to conduct an attack on Steenbergen under the cover of darkness, taking advantage of the element of surprise.

Since the attack of the GGFG and the CGG that afternoon did, in fact, fail to meet expectations, the reconnaissance patrol of the Algonquin Regiment was sent out. Lieutenant Colonel Bradburn (commanding the Algonquin Regiment) received further instructions from Brigadier Moncel before settling on the details of the attack plan [36].

Tunic of Sergeant Walter Harvey, Support Company, Algonquin Regiment (author's collection).

The plan for the night attack was as follows (see p. 54 for a simplified map of the operation): "B" and "D" Companies were given the objective to secure the tank wall on Oudlandsestraat. Once this objective was secured and the central part of Welberg had been captured, the advance towards Steenbergen via Oudlandsestraat could be resumed. As Welberg is situated at a slightly higher elevation than Oudlandsestraat, it was imperative that Welberg be taken first. Failing that, the enemy would be in a perfect position to observe the advance from the higher elevation in Welberg and direct accurate fire at the Canadian targets.

The plan called for the troops at the bridgehead near the Witte Ruiter bridge and the Handwijzer Café to open fire on the German position near midnight, to create a diversion while the Algonquins conducted their attack.

In this light, it is difficult to understand why the Canadians did not shell and destroy the Cornelius church in Welberg, which would have made an ideal observation post for the Germans. Perhaps the shell hits on the church were evidence of a failed attempt. Actually, the tower was not essential to the Germans. In the woods near the Eekelenberg farm (see Map IX on p. 60), a number of trees had been provided with wooden platforms and rudimentary wooden ladders. These observation posts provided an excellent overview, as good as or better than the view from the church tower. For their part, the Germans also had reason to blow up the tower, because it served as an easily identifiable point for artillery from which to correct. Despite all this, the tower survived the war.

Concurrent with the advance of "B" and "D" Coys along Oudlandsestraat, the Algonquin plan saw "A" and "C" Coys advancing to the small chapel on Hoogstraat via the farm known as "The Lantern" (see Map VIII, p. 60). "A" Coy would then secure the centre of Welberg and "C" Coy would push on towards Molenweg. The attack was to be

The small chapel on Hoogstraat as it was before the war. The demolished chapel was rebuilt after the war. (collection C. Slokkers).

supported by the 19th Field Regiment (SP) RCA, which would be in a position to shell Welberg from their location at Vrederust near Bergen op Zoom. Also, Molenweg (W14) would be a target for harassing fire, to be supplied by the 7th Medium Regiment RCA (5.5 inch). Oral sources report that Welberg itself received only sporadic harassing fire and there is no evidence to suggest that an extensive, preparatory artillery bombardment took place.

The four companies would be reinforced by a section of engineers from 8 Field Squadron. At dawn, once "A" and "C" Coys were in position, No. 2 Troop of No. 1 Squadron, Canadian Grenadier Guards (led by Lieutenant MacKinnon) and "C" Coy of the Lake Superior Regiment would be sent ahead to provide support [45].

Welberg itself looked like a ghost town. The streets were deserted. The residents had either taken the advice of the Germans and fled, or were hiding in their shelters. Oddly, not a single German was in sight either. The German guns that had been positioned on Wipstraat the previous day had disappeared.

Just before the attack was due to commence, the Algonquins were dropped off by troop-carrying trucks in the outskirts of Moerstraten. They arrived at the bridgehead over the Oudlandse Waterweg early in the evening, on foot. The company commanders met for a final conference with the officers of the Canadian Grenadier Guards and the Lake Superior Regiment to exchange information. Half an hour before the attack was to be launched, the company commanders of the Algonquins briefed their men on the upcoming action. At approximately 2000 hrs on the 31st of October, the Algonquins gathered at their start line for the night attack.

Sector Oudlandsestraat

The advance of "B" and "D" Coys of the Algonquins along Oudlandsestraat initially proceeded without incident. At 2300 hrs, however, enemy fire erupted near the tank wall. Two German SPGs and a machine gun position were identified at the intersection of Hoogstraat and Oudlandsestraat (E11, Map IV). The German mortars were zeroed in on the position near the tank wall and both Algonquin companies suffered a number of casualties. Machine guns and rifles joined the barrage. The Canadian tactical headquarters (in this case simply a scout car equipped with a radio) closely followed the advance and came under a ten-minute artillery concentration from at least eight guns (Cassidy, 188).

Despite the opposition, an attempt was made to push on towards Koolbaantje (E11, Map IV), but the attack was repulsed by effective German artillery fire. Two Germans, part of a group of 54 recently arrived reinforcements, were taken prisoner. The Algonquins made a second attempt to push towards Koolbaantje and around 0325 hrs (1 November), they managed to dig in near the farm of the Luijks family, at the corner of Oudlandsestraat and Hoogstraat.

The strongest German resistance came from the position at the junction of Oudlandsestraat and Koolbaantje (E11, Map IV). During the night, up to three German armoured vehicles were seen operating in that location. In spite of the fierce resistance, the Algonquins continued to advance to their assigned objective.

At 0615 hrs, a request was made for artillery fire to be directed at the German stronghold on Koolbaantje, despite Canadian troops being only 100 metres away [42]. This desperate call seems to indicate that the Germans were mounting a counter-attack. The call for fire was probably initiated around the time the commander of the attack force, Major J. S. McLeod, was hit in the chest by a shell fragment and had to be evacuated. In the ensuing chaos, the two companies pulled back to a position in front of the tank wall and Lieutenant L. Peart assumed command. The Canadians could hear the German reinforcements arrive and it was clear that another German counter-attack was imminent. "B" Coy dug in to await orders and were told to hold there until the situation on the right flank (Welberg) became clear. The attack had stalled at the German defence line (Cassidy, 188).

Sergeant George Caya, "A" Coy, Algonquin Regiment (photo L. Brown).

Sector Welberg

The advance of "A" Coy proceeded according to plan. Resistance along the route as far as the chapel was negligible. A dozen Germans were taken prisoner, most of them found half asleep in their trenches. Up to that point, the attack had succeeded beyond expectation and "A" Coy established its headquarters at the Koch farm on Hoogstraat.

Sergeant George Caya (No. 7 Platoon, "A" Coy, Algonquin Regiment) describes the early stages of the attack in his book *Warpath Days* [48]. The men were proceeding on foot from the "Lantern" farm towards Hoogstraat:

Some of the land was soggy and as we advanced through the fields, we would come upon some enemy trenches. The night was fairly clear and we could see maybe one hundred feet ahead. We travelled mostly in single file and the man in front, upon coming upon a German who was taking a snooze, [would give him] a tap on the shoulder. When the German opened his eyes, the front man would whisper to him "Nix sprieken" [sic], and the German would surrender and be passed down the line towards our rear. We soon had a dozen prisoners and had not fired a single shot.

It was exhilarating work and one could almost think that he was walking on air. But it was not very promising for accumulating souvenirs, for we had no time to search for them. But fear not, it would not be long before the prisoners were searched for guns, grenades, watches, money, etc. Some Germans carried knives in their boot top.

Once we had cleared the slit trenches of German prisoners, we watched some large explosion in Welberg. [...] We heard someone screaming quite clearly and we also heard the sounds of children crying. All night we marched towards De Bogt, clearing several farms of the enemy without too much trouble.

Before long, we arrived at Begoth [sic] where the German troops belonged to the Hermann Goering Division. So far it had been easy, as if we had been invited. But shortly the party would get rough. [48]

A patrol from "A" Company, the Algonquin Regiment, reported around 0100 hrs that a German armoured vehicle had been spotted at the intersection of Wipstraat and Hoogstraat (H10, Map IV).

Buoyed by the relative success of the mission up to that point, "A" Coy, under the command of Major Atkinson, entered Welberg via the houses on Hoogstraat. Skirmishes followed this incursion and Major Stirling (commanding "C" Coy, positioned at the chapel) sent 13 Platoon under Lieutenant Beckett into Welberg. The men of "A" Coy came under heavy defensive fire on Hoogstraat and, for a brief time, became trapped in a barrage of mortar, rifle, and artillery fire. Major Atkinson was hit in the leg by an enemy bullet and was moved to a cellar while his company set up a perimeter around the house. Finally, around 0300 hrs, "A" Coy reported that Welberg had been consolidated and that, according to a patrol in the direction of Molenweg, the route was clear. Major Stirling's *Major Don Atkinson [44]* "C" Company followed "A" Company's route of advance through Welberg towards Molenweg, as planned.

At that moment, communications problems developed and the two companies found they could only contact each other. Neither "B" and "D" Coys at the tank wall nor battalion headquarters could be reached.

Major Stirling learned that Major Atkinson had been wounded and after establishing his platoons (under Lieutenant Gartley and Sergeant MacDougal) and his headquarters in a defensive position in buildings on both sides of the street, he handed over command to the Sergeant-Major (CSM Ken Buffin). Lieutenant Gartley's platoon occupied a position across the bridge on Corneliusstraat (K8, Map IV). The exact location of the other platoon's position is unknown.

Major Keith Stirling (author's coll.)

Major Stirling managed to locate the position of "A" Coy through Lieutenant Waldie of "A" Coy. Major Atkinson was lying in the cellar with his injury to his leg and "A" Coy's Sergeant-Major (Art Fricker) had assumed command. The communication problem was discussed and an attempt was made to fashion a single serviceable radio using the parts of the three radios present (two from the Algonquin companies and one belonging to the Forward Observation Officer[7]). Captain R.J. Roberts of the 19th Field Regiment (SP), along with two assistants, had been assigned to the Algonquins as FOO to direct the artillery fire [39].

Since the attempt to repair the radio did not appear to be successful, Major Stirling sent his batman-runner and a signaller back to Battalion Headquarters on the Oudlandse Waterweg to report that Welberg had been taken, that the tanks and infantry of the Grenadier Guards and the Lake Superior Regiment could push through, and lastly, that the harassing fire aimed at Molenweg could now be redirected towards Steenbergen.

Meanwhile, the leader of No. 13 Platoon (Lieutenant Beckett) reported to Major Stirling that the platoon had suffered several casualties. Major Stirling told him to leave the casualties with "A" Coy HQ and pull the remainder of the platoon back to the position of "C" Coy.

The signallers had no sooner succeeded in repairing one of the radios and sent the message that the Guards and Lake Superior reinforcements could move out, when the Germans mounted a counter-attack supported by two SPGs.[8] The attackers advanced on Welberg from Molenweg via Wipstraat (H6, Map IV). The Canadians responded with counter-fire and managed to separate the supporting German infantry from the armoured vehicles. The attack stalled, and the armoured vehicles retreated in an easterly direction. This counter-attack would have taken place around 0500 hrs.

At this time, Major Stirling decided to go back to see how his platoons were faring. He located No. 13 Platoon (Lieutenant Beckett), and was told that the other platoons had been overrun. No. 13 platoon had two killed and two wounded, who were being attended by a stretcher bearer (probably Private B. Caroll).

---

[7] A Forward Observation Officer (FOO) is an artillery officer who directs the artillery fire from a forward position, communicating by radio (see Appendix I).

[8] As Major Cassidy points out, the companies had become somewhat scattered at this point and control was being lost. The enemy counter-attack occurred at the moment when this disorganization was at its height (189).

Meanwhile, the troops of the Hermann Goering *Fallschirmjäger Ersatz- und Ausbildungs-Regiment* had launched another counter-attack, again supported by mechanized artillery. By now, the time was 0800 hrs on 1 November and the scene was one of utter confusion.

As a result of the second counter-attack, the men of Lieutenant Gartley's No. 14 Platoon found themselves cut off on Corneliusstraat, with the bridge across the Boomvaart (J8, Map IV) under fire. The fleeing soldiers probably headed for a footbridge that existed at that time, situated some ten metres past the concrete bridge in the direction of Bocht. The German-built footbridge was a simple construction of logs covered by planks, and although the latter had disappeared on "Crazy Tuesday," it was still possible to cross the water via the logs. The Lieutenant and a few of his men covered the retreat across the bridge, and the group managed to reach the position of No. 15 Platoon (probably a house at the junction of Hoogstraat and Wipstraat).

Corporal Britt H. Bell was one of the few men of No. 14 Platoon who managed to escape, thanks to the covering fire of Lieutenant Gartley. The book *Those Army Days* describes how he arrived at the battalion headquarters, exhausted and soaking wet. Bell had swum across the Boomvaart and in his panic, had been forced to abandon his weapon and equipment. He was taken to the back of the line to recover, grinning from ear to ear after his terrifying escape [49].

Larry Brown (left) and Britt Bell (center) on leave in England, 1945 (photo L. Brown).

When part of the platoon had fled across the water, the Germans managed to seize the houses on Corneliusstraat and opened fire on the bridge and the Boomvaart. The men who had covered the retreat of their comrades effectively lost their chance to cross the Boomvaart alive. The small group, still cut off on Corneliusstraat, had to find another way to cross the canal. After covering some distance in the direction of Steenbergen, the lieutenant decided to split up the group and attempt to reach the Canadian lines from the rear, via the Boomdijk road. Unfortunately, the Germans spotted them along the way and forced them to surrender.

Janus Geers mentions two Canadian prisoners of war brought in on the morning of 1 November behind the Welbergsedijk. The Germans took the two Canadians to the Geers' shelter, which the family had been forced to abandon. The two men were probably from Lieutenant Gartley's platoon.

Meanwhile, the situation on the other side of the Boomvaart was equally disastrous. Major Stirling, back at "A" Coy HQ and almost surrounded, could hear his men being taken prisoner in front of the house. German soldiers managed to make their way into the house through an adjoining room, but the Major and the few men who remained were able to drive them off, as well as the Germans located in the backyard. The situation had reached a critical point and they decided to make a run for it from the rear of the building. Survivors report that a German SPG poked its muzzle right through the window of a house to convince the Canadians that surrender was their only option.

Most of the men managed to escape by running through the back yards along Hoogstraat, but as Major Stirling fled, the F.O.O.'s signaller with him was hit and became tangled in the barbed wire. He stopped to help him, only to discover that the man (Gunner A.W. Curphey) had been killed. The major was then overpowered by Hermann Goering troops.

The men of "A" Coy were also on the run, including CSM Art Fricker ("A" Coy). CSM Fricker took shelter in a roadside ditch, and although the Germans conducted an extensive search of the houses and backyards for any Canadians who might be hiding there, they did not find him. He was forced to spend the entire day in his uncomfortable hiding place, since six Germans were occupying a slit trench only a few feet from the ditch in which he was hiding and any noise or movement would have revealed his presence. He managed to escape during the night and report to battalion headquarters [1, 45].

The experiences of the Welberg residents

Seventeen Welberg men, women, and children occupied the cellar of headmaster Baartmans' house on Wipstraat (H6, map IV). They included two clerics (Father Oomen, the priest, and Father Kock, the curate, both dressed in a black cassock with a white collar), the priest's housekeeper Janske Gorissen, and the families of Jan Baartmans, Toon van Broekhoven, Louis van Broekhoven, and Christ Gorissen. Both the church and the boys' school had been hit by artillery fire that day. The occupants of the airless cellar prayed as each strike caused the structure to shake on its foundations. The plaster on the walls and the ceiling came down little by little and covered the occupants in a fine, white dust. A quilted blanket had been hung across the cellar window to screen out some of the violence raging outside. The occupants gradually became aware that the noise was the result of their liberators and the Germans fighting in the streets of Welberg.

Father Kock. Murdered by the Germans on 1 November 1944 (author's collection).

When the violence abated a little, Father Kock and Jan Baartmans cautiously made their way upstairs to size up the situation outside. It must have been around 2 a.m. When they reached the side of the house (next to the café), they saw a small group of Canadian liberators and three German prisoners of war, their hands on their steel helmets. One of the Canadians came over, warmly greeted by the curate and Jan Baartmans. Father Kock, who spoke good English, told the Canadian that there were still some Germans on the other side of the Boomvaart. He gestured expansively towards the church steeple and the girls' school. In fact, the presence of German soldiers could not have been more than a suspicion on the part of the curate; having spent all his time in the cellar, he could not have known the exact location of the German positions.

Back in the cellar, the two men excitedly recounted their meeting with the Canadians and told the others that the liberation was at hand. Then the sounds of battle rose again and they all stayed in the cellar to await further developments.

It was at this point that the Germans launched their first counter-attack, which the Canadians managed to repel. The men of "A" Coy were driven back while "C" Coy opened fire. Since the men who spoke with the curate most likely belonged to "A" Coy, it stands to reason that the captured Germans would have regained their freedom and informed their comrades that the curate had been providing the Canadians with information. While the exact circumstances cannot be reconstructed, the Germans reacted with exceptional violence.

When the sounds of fighting died down, an ominous silence fell over the battle zone in Welberg. All talk in the cellar ceased and people waited, wrapped in their own thoughts. This silence was abruptly shattered by the sound of someone kicking in the kitchen door. Witnesses generally agree that this occurred at around five o'clock in the morning. The trapdoor opened, and a German soldier ordered the occupants out of the cellar. With Jan Baartmans leading the way, the others meekly followed. When the group arrived on the main level, sexton Van Broekhoven and Father Kock were subjected to a closer inspection. Both men were dressed in black and they were roughly the same age. Eventually, Father Kock was identified as the "culprit" and pulled out of the group. The German soldier slapped him across the face, yelling abuse, and dragged him off. At the side of the house, the German hit him in the back of the head with his rifle butt. The curate was taken to the café next door, where the Germans continued to torture him. The rest of the group was put against the wall and kept there at gun point.

The sounds of battle grew louder again as the second counter-attack was launched. This was the attack that forced the Canadians to retreat. The fighting in Welberg drowned out the sounds coming from the café where the curate was kept, making it difficult to hear exactly what was happening there. The German soldier who had beaten the curate ordered the frightened people back into the cellar, certain that he had found the right person. Shortly afterwards, all the occupants of the cellar were ordered to leave and head for Steenbergen. As they filed out of Mr Baartmans' house through the front door, they saw the curate lying under the hedge, critically injured. After torturing him in the café, the Germans had stabbed him in the belly with a bayonet and left him for dead. Father Oomen was able to give the curate absolution before the Germans forced him to leave. He and the rest of the group were ordered to make their way to Steenbergen via Wipstraat. The street was under fire and the terrified group fled along the bank of the canal, shells whistling over their heads. They headed for the Charitas hospital on Kleine Kerkstraat in Steenbergen and reached their destination unharmed, although in a state of terror.

When café owner Piet Koch went outside some time later to see what was happening, he found Father Kock lying under the hedge. Barely audible, the curate begged for water, and Koch moistened his lips with a soaked handkerchief. Hendrikus (Harry) Kock died of his wounds in the afternoon of 1 November at the age of 34. Koch moved the curate's body to the porch of the house, his head resting on a rolled-up mat. On Friday 3 November, the Germans allowed a group of Welberg residents to transport the body to the hospital in a handcart. The curate was buried in the grounds of the hospital, resting beside fourteen other war victims [50, 51].

More Welberg residents were hiding on nearby Wipstraat. The cellars under the houses of Willem van Broekhoven (a housepainter) and Kees Bernaards (the butcher) harboured the families of Willem van Broekhoven, Kees Bernaards, and Marijn van Eekelen (from the "Witkruis" farm). The cellars were connected via an opening in the foundation wall. The Van Eekelens, forced by the German defenders to abandon the shelter they had dug, had been invited to share their neighbours' cellar. The cramped space, shared by some fifteen people, was extremely uncomfortable and young Kees van Eekelen disappeared upstairs, having decided that he would prefer to enjoy a night's rest in the butcher's bed. A few minutes after he lay down, he heard the howling of a shell, followed by an enormous explosion as the projectile hit nearby. Shell fragments rattled across the street. Kees's father ran upstairs and vetoed his son's sleeping plans, assisting his son back down into the cellar. During the night of 31 October to 1 November, the occupants of this cellar also had contact with the Algonquin Regiment.

Jan Gladdines and his family were hiding in a makeshift shelter dug in the backyard of their house on Krommeweg (H6, Map IV). The shelter was very primitive and much too small to hold the large number of people who had gathered there, but the intensity of the shelling was such that they had no choice but to remain in the airless, filthy hole. At times, dozen of shells landed every hour. During the brief respites in the shelling, only those who had urgent calls of nature risked leaving the shelter. Some time later, when there was a lull in the artillery fire, the family set out for Steenbergen. En route, son Theo Gladdines was hit in the knee by a shell fragment and the family took him to the hospital. Son Jan Gladdines, however, had stubbornly remained behind in the neighbour's beer cellar. Despite the sounds of battle and the hysterical screams of his panic-stricken neighbour, he had fallen asleep. Then his father returned by bicycle and summoned Jan to join the family at the hospital. Mr Gladdines went on ahead, leaving his son to assist a family from Zeeland who were fleeing to Steenbergen along the same route. To add to their troubles, Jan accidentally pushed the family's elderly grandmother into the canal, cart and all. Fortunately, they were able to fish the old lady out of the water and the journey to the hospital was resumed. Upon his arrival, Jan recognized his father's bicycle in front of the hospital. Horrified, he saw that the frame had been hit by a shell, breaking it clean in two. It finally dawned on him that his father had risked his life coming back to fetch him.

He entered the hospital but was unable to find his family. The corridors were all but impassable, packed with frightened people. The injured and sick had been moved to the basement, under the care of a few members of the nursing staff. Surgery was also performed in the basement, under very primitive circumstances. There was a shortage of medicines, bandages, and above all, water. Only three doctors were available to provide medical care for all of Steenbergen and surroundings. The emergency organization that had been formed specifically for this type of situation had failed to activate: its members simply had not shown up. A number of Steenbergen residents, including members of the O.D.[9], took it upon themselves to transport injured victims to the hospital at the risk of their own lives.

There was no panic in the hospital. Although frightened, people seemed resigned to whatever fate awaited them. Then the roof was hit by shell fire. Flying glass fragments caused serious injuries to an unfortunate man by the name of Piet Hoendervangers, and the impact of the shell rendered the top floor unfit for use, requiring its evacuation. Since the hospital was already filled to capacity, people were moved to the basement of the Catholic presbytery on Grote

---

[9] The O.D. (Orde Dienst) was a resistance group established by Dutch ex-military for the purpose of imposing and maintaining order immediately following the liberation.

Kerkstraat. Jan Gladdines ended up there as well and awaited the liberation in the company of many other residents of Steenbergen and several German deserters.

On Oudlandsestraat, Willem Mulders was fatally hit by a shell fragment. He was only 54 years old when he died.

Sector Witte Ruiter

October 31st also saw heavy fighting further to the west, near the Witte Ruiter bridge. The bridgehead across the Ligne river had been evacuated on the evening of 30 October, as described. Around 0700 hrs the next morning, a second attempt was made to liberate Steenbergen using this route. The history of the previous day repeated itself. Once again, the soldiers of the Lake Superior Regiment came under heavy defensive fire as soon as they crossed the bridge, and the anti-tank fire from the positions along Bergse Grintweg caused casualties. A request for supporting fire received a rapid response and Canadian shells shrieked off in the direction of the hamlet of Waterhoefke and vicinity, south of Steenbergen, to break the German resistance.

Private Francis Richard ("C" Coy, Lake Superior Regiment) was awarded the DCM. (Distinguished Conduct Medal) for his bravery at the bridgehead. When the platoon commander and his second-in-command were wounded and evacuated, he took command of the platoon on his own initiative. In spite of heavy defensive fire from the Germans, he and the men under his command stayed at their post and successfully defended the position.

Lieutenant Zimmerman, commanding the group of engineers tasked with erecting a bridge across the Ligne river, undertook another reconnaissance tour of the bridgehead. He sustained a minor head injury from a flying shell fragment and his conclusion was not very positive: the fighting made it impossible to construct a bridge without incurring an unacceptable number of casualties.

At the bridgehead, the Canadian soldiers once again heard the rumbling of German tank engines. The platoon commander at the bridgehead reported that his troop strength was insufficient to sustain the attack. Several men had been wounded by sniper and machine gun fire. In response, a

Private Francis Richard (DCM.), Lake Superior Regiment (author's collection)

number of tanks from the Foot Guards made their way to the bridge to support the infantry, in the hope that the tank guns would be able to suppress the enemy fire. The plan was to position the tanks east of the road bordering the Ligne river. Just as on the previous day, the idea was doomed to failure because the tanks' ability to manoeuvre was severely hampered by the numerous trees and ditches and the soggy ground. In spite of these constraints, several tanks continued to provide support as best they could.

The situation did not improve as the day went on. On the contrary: the Foot Guards reported around 1530 hrs that the infantrymen were exhausted and that fresh troops were urgently required. Ammunition, water, and rations were running out. At 1600 hrs, the brigade ordered the infantry to hold their position for the time being, in spite of the arduous circumstances. By now, the tanks had retreated again since the situation was too dangerous and they were, in any case, unable to provide active support. The men in their slit trenches were abandoned for a second time.

The urgent call for relief was finally answered a few hours later. A company of the Lake Superior Regiment located at the hamlet of Oudemolen was ordered to the bridgehead to relieve the troops, who had been under fire all day. The German defensive fire delayed the relief troops' arrival at the bridgehead until after 1800 hrs.

That evening around 2200 hrs, the 4th Armoured Division received the welcome news that the troops of the 10th Infantry Brigade would take over the attack on Steenbergen. The exhausted men of the 4th Brigade were to be pulled back from the front line.

The soldiers at the bridgehead near the Witte Ruiter bridge heaved a sigh of relief at the prospect of finally escaping this sector that had been under continuous fire. As they prepared to make a stealthy departure, however, the Foot Guards launched an artillery barrage in support of the Algonquins' night attack on Welberg. This, in turn, led to an intensification of the German defensive fire, forcing the men at the bridgehead to wait until the situation calmed down. It was not until dawn that they finally found themselves in a position to evacuate the bridgehead without taking further casualties. The soldiers of the Lake Superior Regiment dug in on the Halsteren side of the Ligne. Later that day (1 November), they were relieved by a company of the Argyll and Sutherland Highlanders.

The engineers of 8 Field Squadron RCE were relieved that evening by their colleagues from the 9th Field Squadron RCE. The engineers of the 8th had to support the infantry in Welberg and on Oudlandsestraat. In the end, it was the men of No. 1 section, 9 Field Squadron, who successfully erected the Bailey bridge. Private McInnis lost his leg to a mine during its construction. It is not known exactly when the work was commenced, but it probably started as soon as the Germans left the sector. The bridge was already open to traffic on the morning of 4 November.

Private Jack Graham (B Company, Lake Superior Regiment) was killed that day between Oudemolen and Kladde, after the armoured vehicle in which he was riding hit a mine. The incident injured three other men. Gunner Walter "Chick" Sills of the 23rd Field Regiment (SP) suffered an injury to his leg. He was part of the forward observation team in the front line of the Lake Superior Regiment, probably commanded by Major Telford [14, 13].

Sector Glymes / Kladde

The situation in Lepelstraat had not changed from the previous day. The village was still in a sort of no-man's land between the fronts. The Canadians were situated near the De Handwijzer café and west of Halsteren, while the Germans occupied their line in Westland, Kladde, and Glymes.

The Governor General's Foot Guards dispatched another patrol (Sergeant Arnot) that day in the direction of Lepelstraat / Kladde to reconnoitre the German positions. They encountered a roadblock but managed to skirt it following directions from Sergeant Arnot, who had dismounted from his tank to inspect the obstacle. A short distance past the roadblock, at the hamlet of De

Waterkant near Lepelstraat (G16), the patrol came under fire from the Germans at the Glymes pumping station. Machinegun fire rattled as a German anti-tank gun disabled one of the reconnaissance tanks, hitting its track. Fortunately, no one was injured. Later that day, the disabled tank was retrieved by an armoured recovery vehicle accompanied by six reconnaissance tanks to provide suppressive fire. Evidently, the enemy was still vigorously defending the western flank [36, 14].

ENEMY COUNTER-ATTACK—FIRST BATTLE OF WELBERG

Drawing by Major Cassidy. Copied from the regimental history of the Algonquin Regiment entitled Warpath. The Story of the Algonquin Regiment 1939–1945 *by G. L. Cassidy [1]. Note the Canadian soldiers prone by the side of the road, bottom left corner of the drawing. A corner of the author's house is visible on the extreme right.*

Wednesday 1 November 1944 dawned with a fairly heavy ground fog. The mist dissipated around 9 a.m. but the sky remained heavily overcast. In the evening, the clouds parted, unveiling a bright moon. [35].

The night attack on Welberg had turned into a fiasco. The companies at the tank wall, unable to silence the German mortars, had retreated with their wounded. The German counter-attacks had forced "A" and "C" Coys of the Algonquins to flee Welberg. It is not clear why the reinforcements of the Grenadier Guards and the Lake Superior Regiment did not advance that morning, as had been planned. The only references found in the historical records consulted mention enemy shelling and the inability to advance "due to obstacles." [42].

A total of 27 men from the battalion had been taken prisoner, including four wounded. Eleven of the men who managed to escape had been wounded. Five men were killed in the centre of Welberg: one gunner and four Algonquins. One of the four Canadian casualties lay in a shallow hole in front of a house at the intersection of Wipstraat and Hoogstraat. The body was moved to Hoogstraat some time on 2 November. Four of the Canadian casualties were buried side by side on Hoogstraat, where they remained until just after the liberation. The body of the gunner, A.W. Curphey, has never been found. His name is engraved on the Groesbeek Memorial, situated 10 km south of Nijmegen

General von Zangen, commander of the German 15th Army, mentions the counter-attack near Welberg in his situation report of 2 November [37]:

[...] *Raum 67 A.K. stellte Lage suedl. STEENBERGEN und am Bahn BREDA – DORDRECHT trotz staerkstem Artl-Feuer im Gegenangriff her. Ich spreche den Korps meine Anerkennung aus* [...]

[...] In the operational area of 67 Corps south of Steenbergen and at the Breda - Dordrecht railroad track, successful counter-attacks were mounted in spite of heavy artillery fire. The Corps deserves my highest appreciation [...]

The Algonquins lick their wounds

The Algonquins consolidated their position at their original start line and a period of relative quiet ensued. Back at the bridgehead on the Oudlandse Waterweg, "A" and "B" Coys, having lost a number of men, were consolidated under the command of Captain A. Herrington. They dug in and spent the night of 1/2 November in miserable conditions. The companies were positioned in a line stretching roughly east and west of the "Lantern" farm, with a few SPGs of the 5th Anti-Tank Regiment RCA to render assistance in case of a German attack. Not a single slit trench stayed dry and the men grew chilled to the bone. Sergeant Caya (No. 7 Platoon, "A" Coy, Algonquin Regiment) describes his experiences in the Welberg polder:

We were told that we would be carrying [out] another assault on Welberg soon. Personally, I was ready to go before another night saw us in those miserable slits. One could almost call them water containers. That afternoon, we knew it would soon be time for a flight of Typhoons that would give Welberg a going over with five-hundred pound bombs, and they usually did a good job of it. There was no shortage of cigarettes and at times, they were free. I tried smoking two or more at a time to see if the smoke would warm me up but it only made me sick. I would have given my back pay to be back home with my mom in our little log cabin some twenty miles west of Hearst, catching and eating snow shoe rabbits. [48]

The occupants of the Koolen family's shelter received a visit from a lone Canadian scout that night. The shelter, dug into the Dwarsdijk, also harboured the Koenraadt family, grandfather Hermus, and the De Weert family. The soldier had approached in complete silence and suddenly appeared at the entrance to the shelter, a finger to his lips, urging the occupants of the cellar to keep quiet. Speaking in a whisper, he asked if they knew where the Germans were. One of the occupants spoke English and told the soldier about the German command centre on the farm across the road. The soldier departed as silently as he had come, making his way back to the Canadian lines via the ditch in the fields of the New Kromwiel polder.

That same night, another patrol made its way unseen to the hamlet of Bocht. The sounds they heard told them that the Germans were reoccupying the positions around the Eekelenberg farm and that reinforcements were arriving. The enemy was not ready to give up.

The Geers family on the Pomphoeve farm also discovered that the woods were being reoccupied. Their shelter consisted of a narrow trench covered with logs and a layer of soil, situated in front of the house. Janus Geers, who had become the proud father of a fourth child a few months earlier, left the shelter to fetch fresh diapers for the baby. The barn was heavily damaged by a direct hit but the house was intact. Coming in through the door, he was shocked to find unexpected guests. A small group of Germans sat at the table heating alcohol with vanilla, a potion they were evidently consuming in liberal amounts. The men were dirty and unshaven and, above all, dead drunk. Pointing a pistol at the farmer's chest, the Hermann Goering soldiers ordered Geers out of his house.

The fate of the prisoners of war

The twenty-seven captured Algonquins were taken to the German headquarters in Welberg. Major Keith Stirling estimated that the Germans numbered approximately 120 men equipped with two SPGs. The major was taken to Battalion Headquarters in Steenbergen in a captured jeep which, the Germans told him, had just been confiscated from a captured "general." They were probably referring to Brigadier Thicknese of the 59th AGRA (Army Group Royal Artillery), who set out on a reconnaissance patrol south of Bergen op Zoom armed with a 1:100.000 map and, not surprisingly, lost his way. From Steenbergen, the major and a group of fellow prisoners were taken by truck to the German regimental headquarters (likely in Dinteloord). The group was almost complete again when the Germans started their interrogation. Major Stirling still had a map and field notes in his pocket and was looking for a way to hide these valuable documents. His chance came when he was taken to a neighbouring house with a few of his companions to enjoy a cup of coffee. Sitting on the floor, Private Carroll (the company medic) managed to distract the German guard while the map and notebook disappeared unseen under the rug.

The major was given a cheese sandwich and coffee during the interrogation. Most of the German questions remained unanswered because the major refused to provide his interrogator with military intelligence. The interrogator then turned to the poor relations between the Canadians, the British, and the Americans. To settle that discussion, Major Keith Stirling pulled out a letter he had recently received from Canada. The interrogator was shocked to learn from the letter that Canada was raising two additional divisions to contribute to the war with Japan. Apparently, he had not expected Canada to be eager to play such a major part in the war.

Major Stirling noted down the names of all prisoners of war in his diary [45]:

Major	A.K.J. Stirling	Private	L. Bachmeier
Sergeant	G.T. Costello	Private	M.A. Peterson*
Sergeant	R.E.G. Egerton	Private	R. Beaulieu
Private	A.M. Brownlee	Private	R. Emery
Private	A.W. Wilson	Private	R.K. Butcher
Private	B.C. Carroll	Private	W.E. Cox
Private	C.G. Downs*	Private	W.O. Brooks*
Private	E.H.J. Pegelo	Major	D. Atkinson*
Private	F. Chambers	Lieutenant	K.M. Gartley
Private	F.D.Buckingham	Lieutenant	R.G. Waldie
Private	F.G. Bowes	Corporal	F.P. Weegar
Private	Freisen*	Corporal	R.C. Whitbread
Private	J.W. Blake	Corporal	W.J. Brisbois
Private	J.W. Hudson		

The names marked with an asterisk refer to those who were wounded when they were taken prisoner. Private Freisen is listed as wounded in Major Stirling's diary, but the name is not listed in the regimental archive.

The interrogator then turned to the unfortunate night attack. Since he had already spoken with the rest of the men, he knew most of the details. The only inaccuracy the major heard was that the German thought the Algonquins had already been in Steenbergen, whereas a patrol from "A" Coy had advanced no further than halfway up Wipstraat. When the interrogation ended, the major was taken back to rejoin the others. The temperature in the room was comfortable and while the men warmed up and were given something to eat, the major was taken to yet another house. Its occupants made coffee and prepared sandwiches, which he shared with the guards and his hosts. In the afternoon, the prisoners received a hot meal and were unexpectedly deprived of their watches. With typical German thoroughness, they were given a receipt for the stolen watches and told that they would be reimbursed for the value of their timepieces once they arrived at their final destination. Major Stirling had made no attempt to hide his watch following earlier assurances by the Germans that it would not be confiscated.

A short time later, the men were taken on a three-kilometre march to a canal, where they boarded a boat filled with German wounded. The prisoners were transported to Dordrecht (probably via Dintelsas), where they stayed for three days and were subjected to further interrogations. Finally, they were transported to Germany, where they awaited the end of the war in a prisoner-of-war camp. Major Stirling spent his time in *Oflag* 79, an officers' camp near Brunswick in Lower Saxony. Living conditions in the POW camps were so poor that when the major arrived back in Canada, he weighed only forty kilos (97 lbs). His time in the camp had severely affected his health and he died too young, at the age of 51 [45].

German media photo taken in Steenbergen on 1 November on what is known today as Watertorenweg. Two Canadian prisoners are marched under guard past a German self-propelled assault gun (collection J. van Doorn)

The people at home did not learn the fate of their relatives until several months later. In the case of Sergeant Terence Costello, an article finally appeared in the Hamilton Spectator on 23 January 1945:

Sgt Terence Costello, son of George Costello, 4 Longwood Road North, has been officially reported a prisoner of war in Germany after action in Holland in November. During the action in which the Algonquin Regiment, along with other Canadian forces, was trying to take Welberg and Bocht, Sgt Costello was wounded when a piece of shrapnel lodged in his back. His company was ordered to withdraw. He stayed to assist in evacuating the wounded and was captured by the enemy. It was later learned that he, along with the other prisoners, was evacuated to Germany. On November 15, his parents received a card from their son stating that he was a prisoner of war and was interned at Stalag camp11B. A radio dispatch from the German European Service reported him a prisoner December 8, 1944, and this report was confirmed by Allied sources last Friday. [53]

A further article about Sergeant Costello appeared on 16 April 1945, some time after he had been liberated from the POW camp and had reached England. The other captured soldiers were also liberated in April 1945 and eventually repatriated.

The 10th Infantry Brigade takes over the attack

On the evening of 31 October, a decision was made at the division level to withdraw the 4th Armoured Brigade from the Oudlandsestraat sector and to use the 10th Infantry Brigade to break through the German defence.

Accordingly, "C" Coy, Argyll and Sutherland Highlanders of Canada (commanded by Captain S.D. Chapman), relieved No. 1 Squadron of the Canadian Grenadier Guards and "C" Coy of the Lake Superior Regiment at the bridgehead over the Oudlandse Watergang. The relief took place at 1800 hrs. The new company evidently encountered major difficulties, since they were relieved shortly afterwards by the Argylls' carrier platoon, having suffered two casualties (wounded) during the brief period they spent at the bridgehead. The carrier platoon in their armoured vehicles were better protected against the mortar shell fragments.

The bridgehead over the Ligne river at the Witte Ruiter bridge was abandoned after midnight, as previously described. The men had dug in near the tank wall on the Halsteren side of the Ligne. The Lake Superior Regiment and the Foot Guards regrouped on 1 November in Heerle for a brief period of rest. The Foot Guards were relieved by tanks of the South Alberta Regiment, while the Argylls relieved the Lake Superior infantry.

Although unconfirmed by the written sources consulted, it is likely that this bridgehead was abandoned once and for all. After 1 November, not a single source mentions any action at the bridgehead.

Plans for a new attack

In spite of the major setbacks, the Algonquins lost no time in conducting extensive patrols on Wednesday 1 November. The scouts and the carrier platoon concentrated on the eastern sector, in the direction of the Boomdijk, and it is likely that the nocturnal encounter between a Canadian soldier and the Koolen family mentioned above involved a member of one of these groups. The patrols determined that the area could be reached without difficulty from Krabbenweg (Q15) to the junction of the Dwarsdijk and the Boomdijk (P14).

The plan for a second attack on Welberg was worked out in detail by the staff of the 10th Infantry Brigade. For unknown reasons, Welberg was retained as the main axis of the attack. Instead of an attack by one (weakened) battalion, a complete brigade, including support troops, would now be thrown into the fray.

The Lincoln and Welland Regiment was deployed in the Oudlandsestraat sector at the tank wall. Its objective was to advance to Hoogstraat and enter Steenbergen via Oudlandsestraat. The Algonquin Regiment was deployed in the Boomdijk/Groenedijk sector, with the objective to secure Welberg via the same route. The Argylls were kept in reserve. Depending on the success of the attack, they would be deployed as required. Self-propelled anti-tank guns (M10 "Achilles" Tank destroyers) of the 5th Anti-Tank Regiment RCA had also been assigned to the infantry for support. Their mission was to destroy the German SPGs. The "Rainbow Battery" (14th Anti-

Tank Battery) was assigned to the Lincoln and Welland Regiment, while the 96th Anti-Tank Battery was placed under the command of the Algonquin Regiment.

Self-propelled anti-tank gun of the 96th Battery, 5th Anti-Tank Regiment, of the type used in Welberg [10].

Elements of the South Alberta Regiment and the New Brunswick Rangers (13th Independent Machinegun Coy, armed with heavy mortars and Vickers machine guns) had also been allocated to support the infantry. "A" Squadron of the South Albertas was placed under the command of the Algonquin Regiment for the action and "B" Squadron under that of the Lincoln and Welland Regiment.[10] As of 3 November, two troops of the Fife and Forfar Yeomanry were also available for support. This unit was equipped with "Crocodile" flame-throwing tanks, which were deployed on the evening of 3 November to support the Argylls. The flame-throwing equipment was not used, however.

Engineer platoons were assigned to the attack troops to clear the multitude of mines. Prior to the attack, they were fully occupied clearing the access roads. They also filled in a large crater in the Boomdijk road that day (at the junction of the Boomkanaal and the Oudlandse Watergang). One section of engineers cleared Boswijkdreef of 88 Teller mines (T.Mi.42 – plate-shaped German anti-tank mines). A number of these mines were found buried in pairs, stacked one on top of the other.

---

[10] The actions of this squadron are referred to in the regimental history of the Lincoln and Welland Regiment [8], although the author of this work does not identify the unit as "B" Squadron. The squadron is described as having played an important part in destroying German strongholds during the early morning of November 3rd. No other written sources have been located.

To support the attack, the artillery was moved into position in the vicinity of Halsteren. As mentioned, the 19th Field Regiment RCA was positioned near Vrederust north of Bergen op Zoom. The 15th Field Regiment RCA was to Halsteren, north of Bergen op Zoom, and the 7th Medium Regiment RCA was also available for the attack. They took up their positions on 1 November, just across the Zoom river north of Bergen op Zoom.

An Air Observation Post had also been assigned to the attack, to assist in directing fire from the air. The pilot and an artillery observation officer patrolled the Steenbergen front in a two-seater, single-engine Auster. It is interesting to note that according to an eye witness report, not a single German fired at the small aircraft. Firing meant betraying one's position, and that would undoubtedly have resulted in quick action, reducing their artillery piece to a smoking wreck [1, 25, 35].

British pilots of the Artillery Air Observation Squadron that supported the 4th Armoured Division in the battle of Welberg. This photo was taken in late November 1944 (PA 113669).

The rainfall had made it difficult for the 15th Field Regiment RCA to find a suitable position. The soft, muddy ground was a major problem, since each recoil would cause the guns to sink further into the ground. This reduced the accuracy of their aim, which in turn raised the likelihood of shells falling on friendly troops to an unacceptable level. The regiment eventually found a firmer, sandy piece of ground along the main road and deployed in that location. Large piles of ammunition were stored under the shelter of the trees. Watched with fascination by members of the local population, the gunners commenced firing in the direction of Steenbergen. Tragically, one of the artillery shells hit a low-flying Allied bomber on its way back to England, causing it to crash in the polder behind Lepelstraat [12].

The guns remained active all night and harassing fire was directed at the German defence line below Steenbergen in preparation for the coming attack. This shelling cost Adriaan de Jong (44) his life as he left his shelter on the Welbergsedijk. Jacobus Ligtenberg (51) died that same day, hit by artillery fire on the Bergse Grintweg. Rochus Brouwers of Oudlandsestraat died a few days later in Bergen op Zoom from the injuries he received during the bombardments.

Thursday 2 November was a clear, cloudless day. In the evening, it began to rain. The rainfall continued until Friday morning [35].

Fleeing to Moerstraten

Farmer Geers of the Pomphoeve farm, who had fled back to his shelter after his adventure with the drunken Germans in his house on the previous day, had been joined by old Mr Koch from across Hoogstraat. Mr Koch had made his way in the dark across the fields to the Geers' shelter, accompanied by his two sons. He said he had spoken with some Canadians during the night and that they had given him cigarettes. As mentioned previously (p. 33), "A" Coy briefly had its HQ on the Koch farm. Mr Koch proposed that they should all set off in the direction of the liberators. He was certain that there would be another attack by the Canadians, and with good reason.

Farmer Geers and his wife and four children (including the baby) and Mr Koch and his two sons left the shelter around 0900 hrs. They took a crossroad to make their way to the Lantern farm. The road was deserted but strewn with abandoned military equipment, including helmets, shoes, belts, and the like. Deep trenches had been dug on both sides of the road. When they got halfway, weapons opened up on both sides. Bullets whizzed through the trees and kicked up dirt. Mr Koch urged the group to keep going, to avoid giving the invisible gunners the impression that they were soldiers seeking cover. After enduring some terrifying moments under fire, the group arrived unharmed at the Lantern farm owned by Mr Loos. Since the shelter there was full, the group decided to continue on to Moerstraten via Oudlandsestraat. Along the way, they encountered other people trying to flee the violence. Most had left their homes in haste, taking with them only a few of their most valuable possessions. The road was crowded with families pushing small handcarts piled high with their belongings, hurrying fearfully down the road to escape the danger.

Moerstraten was a hive of activity. The village was bursting at the seams with trucks, tanks, and armoured vehicles. Muddy ambulances arriving from the direction of Welberg had difficulty manoeuvring through the narrow main street leading to Bergen op Zoom. Each time one of the vehicles turned a corner, the bright red trail of blood left behind grew longer ...

The situation among the residents of Koolbaantje

The Helmons family, hiding in their shelter, had already suffered through two days and two nights of fighting. At 5 p.m. that day, the German officer who had been keeping tabs on the number of people in the shelter returned once more. He ordered the family to flee to a safer location. To add force to his order, he said: "Es war nur Kinderspiel," [this was only child's play], referring to the activities over the past few days in comparison with the impending Canadian attack. Dirty and exhausted and above all frightened, the family emerged from their shelter to seek safety in flight. The German had already disappeared and no one knew where to go. The reinforced positions along Bergse Grintweg had been stripped of their camouflage and were clearly visible, as were a number of German SPGs positioned along the same road. As the Helmons made their way towards the main road, they were stopped by the Germans and forced to retrace their steps, so they turned towards Hoogstraat. At the corner of Oudlandsestraat and

Hoogstraat (E11, Map IV), they encountered a German officer in full uniform standing in the middle of the intersection, binoculars to his eyes, observing the situation near the tank wall and seemingly oblivious to the bullets whizzing past his ears. The German officer gruffly ordered the family (parents and 6 children) to turn back. This route was clearly not an option either. Back on Koolbaantje, they passed the Nijssen family's shelter, which had earlier been requisitioned by the Germans. That had turned out to be a blessing in disguise, since a direct hit had completely destroyed the shelter. Two dead Germans and five moaning wounded were lying in the ruins. The Roelands family had suffered a shell hit immediately behind their shelter, and the force of the explosion had sent items of clothing flying through the air. The fluttering remnants of shirts and pants festooning the trees formed a sinister decoration.

The Helmons finally fled towards Molenweg along Oudlandsestraat and headed for Notendaal via Olmendreef (C9, Map IV). Just before they reached the Ligne river, they came upon two heavy German machine guns dug in beside the road, directing an almost continuous stream of fire towards the Dassenberg estate. A few Germans were standing on the road, watching. They were not exactly the pick of the proud German army. One of them, a short, shabbily dressed man, looked on with complete indifference as he gnawed on a sausage. The tail end of his meal was lying in the dust on the road. The crew of the first machine gun nodded to the Helmons to indicate it was safe to pass. As soon as they had passed, the machine guns resumed their fire and bullets passed so close to the refugees that it made their pant legs flap. They finally reached Notendaal after an otherwise uneventful journey and fell asleep in a pile of hay in a barn. They would not return to the remnants of their house on Koolbaantje until November 4th.

Preparations for the new attack

As indicated previously, Welberg remained the primary axis of the attack. In preparation for the attack, the enemy positions would be subjected to an aerial bombardment and an artillery barrage, after which two infantry battalions would break through the defensive line around Steenbergen. The third battalion would remain in reserve until the breakthrough had been accomplished. Tactically, the plan was as follows: the Lincoln and Welland Regiment would advance from the tank wall on Oudlandsestraat to the junction of Koolbaantje and Bergse Grintweg. The Algonquins were to gain a position at the intersection of Hoogstraat and Wipstraat. Once these positions were consolidated, the Argyll and Sutherland Highlanders would liberate Steenbergen.

The Lincoln and Welland Regiment arrived at the bridgehead over the Oudlandse Watergang at 1400 hrs. They took over the positions of the Algonquin companies that were moving towards the Boomdijk. "B" Coy of the Lincoln and Welland Regiment and the men and vehicles of the 14th Battery of the 5th Anti-Tank Regiment RCA were held in reserve near the farm of the Peeters family. "A" and "C" Coys had been assigned the objective of reaching Koolbaantje and Hoogstraat respectively. "D" Coy had been ordered to follow a more westerly direction, towards Bergse Grintweg. Depending on developments during the advance of the attacking companies, "B" Coy and/or the anti-tank guns could be deployed on either flank. In addition, two sections from No. 3 Troop, 8th Field Squadron RCE, led by Lieutenant A.B. McAdam, were assigned to the Lincoln and Wellands to clear mines.

The Algonquins drew up detailed plans for reaching the objective they had been assigned. New reconnaissance patrols were sent out to double-check the reconnaissance reports of 1 November. The German occupation of the route along the Boomdijk seemed relatively weak and the Brigadier ordered the Algonquins to attack Welberg that same evening. Lieutenant Colonel Bradburn already had a plan in mind. Aerial photographs and maps were brought in to assist with the detailed preparations and the company commanders were brought in one by one to receive their instructions and discuss their objectives.

The objective assigned to the Algonquins' "A" and "B" Coys was to reach the hamlet of Bocht along both sides of the Boomvaart and then occupy two sectors: the sector around the church (code- named "Jock") and the junction of Wipstraat and Hoogstraat (code-named "Don"). "D" Coy under Major Cassidy had orders to enter Welberg from the east via the Dwarsdijk/Groenedijk (objective "Scotty"). The code names were based on the first names of the company commanders who had been wounded or taken prisoner in the preceding episode and who were no longer with the regiment (Don Atkinson, Keith Stirling, etc.). "C" Coy was kept in reserve for the time being so they could reinforce as required. Their subsequent objective was to occupy sector "Keith"—the Welbergsedijk from the Laurentiusdijk to Kromwielswegje.

Given the previous experience with the German mobile artillery, a large number of anti-tank weapons were provided (PIATs - Projectors, Infantry, Anti Tank). The self-propelled 17-pounders of the 5th Anti-Tank Regiment RCA were assigned to the infantry. One troop (four vehicles from "B" Troop, 96th Battery, commanded by Lieutenant Roberts) was assigned to "A" Coy on the left flank, and one troop ("C" Troop, 96th Battery, commanded by Lieutenant Hooke) was kept in reserve for the time being. A section of engineers was added to the force along the Boomdijk. A section of anti-tank guns from the Algonquins' own regiment (6-pounders) was added to "D" Coy. At least one troop of the South Alberta Regiment ("A" Squadron) would remain in reserve during the night and reinforce the attackers at dawn. The battalion also received two sections of No. 3 Troop, 8th Field Squadron RCE. These mine-clearing troops were commanded by Lieutenant H.E. Lake.

The attack was set to commence on Thursday 2 November at 1900 hrs [1].

The aerial bombardment and artillery barrage of Welberg

In preparation for the attack, the German line of defence received the full treatment to "soften it up." At approximately 1700 hrs, 40 fighter-bombers (Typhoon ground-attack aircraft) carried out an attack on Welberg and the southern section of Steenbergen. The targets of the operation, code-named "WINKLE,"[11] were Hoogstraat from Bergse Grintweg as far as Welberg, Corneliusstraat, and the Welbergsedijk up to the polder drainage canal. Molenweg and Krommeweg up to the Lautentiusdijk were also bombed [42]. The 15th Field Regiment RCA in Halsteren fired white smoke grenades at pre-determined positions to identify the targets for the rocket attacks.

The Germans lacked sufficient anti-aircraft guns so that the aircraft were able to skim low over the houses and drop their deadly loads of 500-lb bombs virtually without opposition. The

---

[11] The code name "WINKLE" did not apply specifically to the aerial attack on Welberg. "WINKLE" was a generic term used for a fixed-attack scheme (information J. Van Doorn).

bombs and rockets dropped by the Typhoons caused enormous craters up to eight metres in diameter and up to two metres deep.

The Air Observation plane was overhead during the raid to spot German anti-aircraft guns and coordinate the artillery fire to destroy them. The battle reports state that the artillery observer in the small plane was able to eliminate two anti-aircraft guns in this manner [42].

When the aerial attack had been completed, the Auster reconnaissance plane stayed in the air over Steenbergen. On board was the commander of the 7th Medium Regiment RCA (Lieutenant Colonel F. Haszard), who maintained contact with the fire direction centre of the 10th Infantry Brigade and reported all possible targets. German vehicles were the main objectives but if none were spotted, there were always "suspected" hiding-places that could be shelled. The fire direction centre coordinated the information and transmitted it to the various artillery regiments in Halsteren [32].

The aerial bombardment was followed by an artillery barrage with 25-pounder field artillery and the medium artillery of the 7th Medium Regiment RCA. This was followed in turn by covering fire for the coming attack in a series of concentrated barrages. Two Forward Observation Officers of the 15th Field Regiment RCA had been added to the infantry for fire support during the battle—Captain Griffin to the Lincoln and Welland Regiment on Oudlandsestraat, and Captain Geig to the Algonquin Regiment.

Twelve minutes before the infantry was due to attack, the artillery in Halsteren commenced firing. Nearly all of the southern portion of Steenbergen was reduced to rubble. The shelling continued until 1925 hrs, 25 minutes after the attack was launched.

The violent bombardments cost Adriaan Suijkerbuijk, 75, his life; he was fatally injured on Koolbaantje. Jan Schijvenaars had his leg torn off by a shell. Marijn Buuron evacuated him from the Welbergsedijk to the hospital in Steenbergen, on a handcart. Jan Schijvenaars died of his injuries on 21 November 1944, aged 65.

Bart Gorissen witnessed the shelling and bombardment of Welberg. He and his family lived on Welbergsedijk, just west of Kromwielswegje. Like everyone else, they had constructed a sturdy shelter, located right beside the road. To their dismay, a German SPG that had been directing fire towards the Boomdijk and the Eekelenberg farm from the Welbergsedijk drove right into the shelter before they had a chance to use it. Fortunately, the communal shelter constructed by the people in the neighbourhood still had room for the Gorissen family. Shortly afterwards, a direct hit on the roof of the shelter injured both Kees van Rooi and Tinus Gorissen. Tinus had his thigh ripped open by a shell fragment while Kees sustained a bleeding head wound. During a lull in the shelling, they decided to leave the uncomfortable shelter. The wounded in particular were having a difficult time in the cramped space. They went into the house to have a snack just as the aerial bombardment and the huge barrage over Welberg erupted. Five or more low-flying aircraft thundered over the roofs of the houses, making several passes to drop their rockets and bombs. The Gorissens had just fled into the cellar of their house when a bomb exploded 10 metres away. Both the cellar door and the window blew out of their frames. The concussion wave blew dust, wood splinters, and grit in all directions. The cellar floor seemed to lift half a metre into the air under the heavy explosion. The occupants, in a blind panic, fled back to the communal shelter that had been dug into the soil.

The shelling of Welberg was extremely intense. Entire trees along the dike were ripped out and found afterwards on the opposite side of the dike. The extreme violence of the shelling is illustrated by Leen IJzermans' situation. When he returned to the spot where his house had stood, all he found was an enormous crater. There was not a trace left of his house or any of his

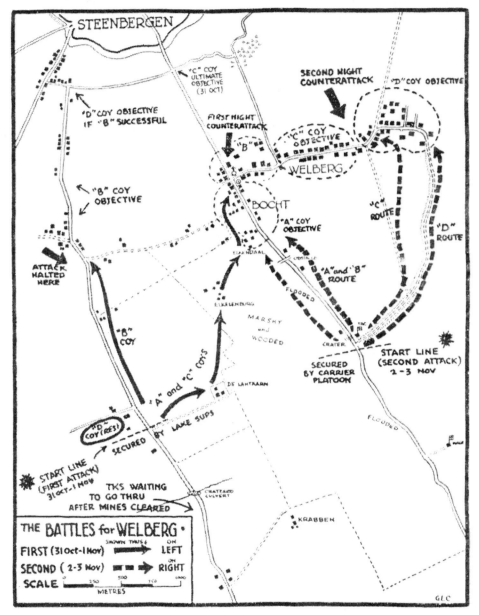

Map VII: *Overview map from "Warpath," the regimental history of the Algonquin Regiment. Both the unfortunate night attack of 31 October and the subsequent attack on 2 November are plotted on the map [1].*

furniture. Everything he owned had been blown sky-high by a direct hit, pulverized into a million pieces, and scattered across a wide area.

While the preparatory barrage hit Welberg and Oudland, the companies advanced along the Boomdijk road towards Welberg. In the evening light, the Canadian soldiers saw the horizon glow red from the exploding shells. The noise stupefied the senses and the air was filled with acrid gun smoke. The second attack on Welberg had begun.

Sector Boomdijk

"A" Coy of the Algonquin Regiment (led by Captain Stock) reached the start line together with their attached 17-pounder anti-tank guns from the 5th Anti-Tank Regiment RCA. "B" Coy (led by Captain Johnny Jewell) remained behind at the junction of the Dwarsdijk and the Boomdijk; they would start their advance along the Boomdijk a short time later. "A" Coy crossed the Boomvaart and moved towards Welberg through the woods, on a course parallel to the canal.

The defenders immediately opened fire. One of the Canadian vehicles became mired in the mud and a huge effort was required to pull the colossus free. The German fire intensified and bullets whizzed across the dike. Canadian progress was very slow, in part because of the small number of soldiers present. "A" Coy numbered 33 men at that point, divided in two sections. Doctrinally, a company in the Canadian army is supposed to have 127 men. Further, almost all the soldiers were new arrivals, to compensate for the losses suffered on the previous day. This meant that few of the men had combat experience. Oral sources report that a group of very young and very frightened soldiers were receiving training for the coming attack on the Oerlemans farm on Krabbenweg. The boys were evidently being prepared for the worst, since they were receiving instructions in the use of the bayonet. Bales of hay served as opponents.

Captain Stock was unable to spread out his men as he was hemmed in on both sides by water: the Boomvaart on the right, and flooded land on the left. This left the men even more exposed to the defensive fire from the Germans. At 2045 hrs, a German SPG in Welberg took aim at the attackers. An M10 tank destroyer was hit half an hour later and caught fire. The flames illuminated the attackers, making their silhouettes clearly visible to the Germans, and a stream of accurately aimed fire brought the attack to a complete halt. The burning tank was located close to the Eekelenberg farm, in the woods. Only one man managed to escape the burning wreck alive, despite the injuries to his hip and leg. Four of his comrades (Sergeant M.R. Koll, soldiers M.S. Desjardin, D.L. Minion and A.S. McLellan) perished in the flames. A second tank, some twenty metres ahead, found itself blocked by the burning wreck and was unable to retreat. Soon afterwards, this tank was also put out of action and destroyed by fire. Fortunately, no lives were lost in this case as the crew managed to escape in time [43]. The second tank was positioned in the yard of the Eekelenberg farm (the Loos family).

The story goes that some children playing in the wreck of the first tank after the battle was over received the shock of their lives when they discovered a shoe inside that still contained a foot. Several months after the liberation, a human hand, covered in blisters, was found a few metres in front of the tank.

The attackers retreated around midnight to their starting position on the Boomdijk. The retreat nearly degenerated into a headlong flight and it was only with great difficulty that Captain Stock managed to stop the frightened newcomers from succumbing to panic. The German defence had proven too strong for the inexperienced attackers.

"B" Coy's efforts on the Boomdijk were equally fruitless. A huge crater in the road just past the start line blocked the way for any vehicles of the 5th Anti-Tank Regiment RCA. The road beyond the crater was strewn with mines, which impeded the advance. "B" Coy had no option but to dig in at the start line to protect themselves from the German defensive fire [1].

Sector Dwarsdijk

The advance of "D" Coy of the Algonquin Regiment under Major George Cassidy proved to be less problematic. They followed the Dwarsdijk road to the junction with the Groenedijk road (P12-13). Here, they temporarily parked the carriers and 6-pounder anti-tank guns.

That is probably the moment when Piet Snoeijers joined the Canadians. He and his family lived at that location. The story goes that he asked for a helmet and a rifle to join the soldiers in their battle. He was probably accompanied by Piet Augustijn. Together, they conducted reconnaissance along the Groenedijk. It is not clear whether they worked on their own initiative or in cooperation with the Algonquins. Piet Snoeijers was found afterwards in a ditch at the end of the Groenedijk, critically injured. He died of his wounds at the age of 18 in a hospital in Antwerp.

Since the right flank of the Groenedijk was undefended, a section was positioned along the dike to provide flank security. The land east of the Groenedijk was mostly under water, so the chance of a German attack from that direction was minor.

With all the noise coming from the Boomdijk, the German defenders were probably unable to hear the men of "D" Coy. No defensive fire was encountered until three hundred metres before the built-up area, when a machine gun opened fire. Corporal Wes Callander sent a volley in reply and his aim was so accurate that he hit the machine gunner in the head, as they found out afterwards. Two platoons were now in a position to check out the first houses on the Welbergsedijk.

According to eyewitnesses, a section of Germans was entrenched in the small house of the Iriks family at the junction of the Groenedijk and the Welbergsedijk roads (P12). A fire exchange took place with the Canadians on the Groenedijk, with additional German harassing fire from the woods on the other side of the Boomvaart, as described. The Iriks family and approximately fourteen other people were hiding in their shelter when a large shell fragment cut straight through the roof and embedded itself in Ariaan Iriks' leg. Another man by the name of De Weert sustained a wound in his arm. Local resistance members Koos Veraart and Piet Lammeree carried the injured Ariaan Iriks off on an improvised litter. The heavy shelling forced the two stretcher bearers to take shelter on the corner of the Laurentiusdijk (H8, Map IV), while the unfortunate casualty remained in the open and was pelted by tiles blown off a nearby roof. When he finally reached the hospital in Steenbergen, it was filled beyond capacity and there was no room for him. After a circuitous, lengthy, and very painful journey, Ariaan Iriks finally wound up in the hospital of Antwerp. Meanwhile, the Iriks family had fled their shelter in a panic and sought refuge in the barn across the street, owned by Rikus van Terheijden, until a German took up position in the barn. Fearing Canadian fire aimed at the German's position, they fled once more and headed for the Vierhoeven farm, past the polder drainage canal.

The Canadians took three prisoners when they arrived at the junction of the Groenedijk and Welbergsedijk. Major Cassidy ordered the rest of his troops to advance along the dike road. When the first vehicle turned into the built-up area of Welberg, a German fired his *pantzerfaust*.

The projectile missed its target, hit a barrow of turnips, and exploded in the air, harming no one. Lieutenant Neil's section routed this small group of defenders in short order. A short distance away on the Welbergsedijk, the platoon came upon a barn harbouring a group of Germans who were offering resistance. CSM Bud McPhee overpowered this position practically single-handedly. One of the prisoners they took was a very young, frightened German officer, who was probably the same officer featuring in Kees van Eekelen's story (p. 65). The Canadians cautiously advanced and at 2100 hrs, objective "Scotty" (Welbergsedijk from Groenedijk to Welbergswegje) was reported held [1, 35].

Sector Oudlandsestraat

At 2000 hrs, an hour after they crossed their start line, "A" Coy of the Lincoln and Welland Regiment adopted positions at the intersection of Hoogstraat and Oudlandsestraat (the Luijks farm, E11, Map IV). "C" Coy had reached the Timmermans farm on the corner of Oudlandsestraat and Koolbaantje (D11, Map IV). "D" Coy occupied a position on the farmland between the "Panhoef" farm of the Van der Heijden family and Waterhoefke (N14).

The "Links and Winks" encountered the same problems that had confronted the men of the Algonquin Regiment on the evening of 31 October. The German mortars and small-arms fire caused a great many casualties and "A" Coy in particular (led by Captain W.H. Barkman) was hit hard.

At around 2200 hrs, a German SPG opened fire on "D" Coy of the Lincoln and Welland Regiment, commanded by Captain Dickie. According to Captain Dickie's report, the fire came from *behind* the Canadian lines.[12]

An hour later, at approximately 2300 hrs, Captain Dickie took his men back to the Panhoef farm. The accurate fire had made their original position untenable. "A" and "C" Coys were also forced to retreat. They occupied a position right behind the tank wall. The regimental history lists 31 wounded and four killed in this action, which clearly reflects the gravity of the situation [38].

Sector Glymes / Kladde

On 2 November, 101 Battery of the 8th Light Anti-Aircraft Regiment RCA was ordered to reinforce the Canadian line in the Glymes/Kladde sector. The gunners were used as infantrymen on the line near Lepelstraat. Elements of the South Alberta Regiment and the Argylls had arrived in this sector the day before. For additional reinforcement, a platoon of heavy machineguns of the New Brunswick Rangers was added to the gunners. As the sector was reasonably quiet, it was considered an acceptable risk to man the line with soldiers lacking combat experience.

---

[12] At first thought, Captain Dickie's claim appears very implausible, since Oudlandsestraat had been in Canadian hands since 31 October. A resident of Welberg mentioned, however, that a wreck was left behind on Oudlandsdijkje. Given the position of "D" Coy, it was in fact possible to fire on the Canadians in the polder from behind. The wreck may well have been that of the German assault gun, which would confirm Captain Dickie's story. Unfortunately, no other source or witness could be found to confirm the presence of the tank wreck on Oudlandsdijkje.

The men dug chest-high trenches and placed their rifles and some ammunition on a piece of green canvas along the edge. The trenches, placed at irregular intervals, formed a chain that snaked across the terrain. A few heavier weapons were positioned further towards Eendracht, their barrels pointing at Tholen, Vossemeer, and Kladde. Squares of orange cloth were placed just ahead of the positions to warn Allied aircraft of their presence.

During the night, the Germans suddenly opened up with an SPG and mortars, shelling the gunners' defensive line just outside Lepelstraat. Their aim was evidently accurate because they blew up five vehicles. Fortunately, there were no Canadian casualties. As a counter-measure, "E" Troop shelled Kladde with 40 mm Bofors anti-aircraft guns, using high-explosive and armour-piercing ammunition. In the dark, the tracer ammunition provided a macabre display of fireworks, lines of rapidly moving dots of light streaking across the sky towards Kladde. One of the shells hit a barn in Kladde, which went up in flames. The Germans understood the signal and fell silent [31, 18].

Map VIII: 1944 Canadian ordnance map of the Steenbergen/Welberg region.

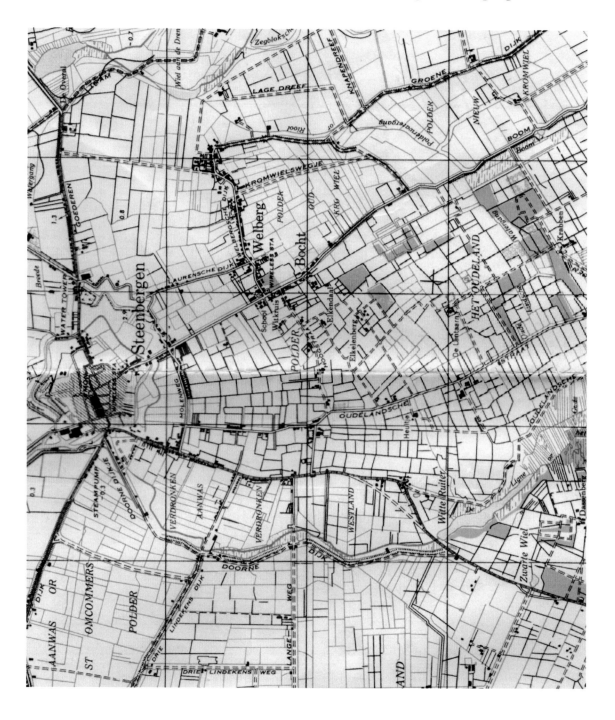

Map IX: *The same 1944 ordnance map with the names of a number of farms and families in the vicinity of Steenbergen and Welberg.*

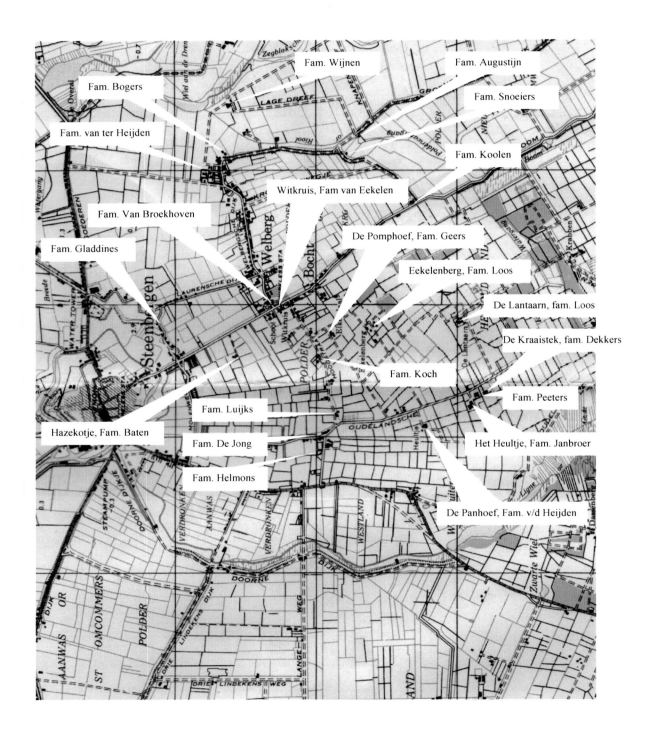

Fam. Wijnen

Fam. Augustijn

Fam. Bogers

Fam. Snoeiers

Fam. van ter Heijden

Fam. Koolen

Witkruis, Fam van Eekelen

Fam. Van Broekhoven

De Pomphoef, Fam. Geers

Fam. Gladdines

Eekelenberg, Fam. Loos

De Lantaarn, fam. Loos

De Kraaistek, fam. Dekkers

Fam. Koch

Fam. Peeters

Fam. Luijks

Hazekotje, Fam. Baten

Fam. De Jong

Het Heultje, Fam. Janbroer

Fam. Helmons

De Panhoef, Fam. v/d Heijden

60

Friday 3 November was a dry day, after a night of continuous rain. The sky remained heavily overcast [35].

Sector Boomdijk

"A" and "B" Coys of the Algonquin Regiment, under heavy fire, had been forced to retreat to the start line at the junction of the Dwarsdijk and the Boomdijk (P14), as mentioned. "B" Troop of 96 Battery, 5th Anti-Tank Regiment RCA, had only one operational M-10 left. Two of the tank destroyers had been gutted in the fighting and one was still stuck in the mud.

In the morning, the two companies launched another desperate attack but were forced to take cover after sustaining several more casualties. The attack was clearly doomed to fail. The only gain that resulted from the attack via the Boomdijk was that it distracted the Germans, which made it easier for "D" Coy to advance along the Welbergsedijk. "A" Coy lost one killed and six wounded in this action.

It was not until mid-afternoon, when the soldiers of "C" Coy reached the Cornelius church, that "A" and "B" Coys were also able to enter Welberg via the hamlet of Bocht. Since the bridge across the Boomvaart canal in Bocht had been blown up, the vehicles obviously could not cross the water and had to advance along the opposite side of the Boomvaart.

The tactical headquarters of the Algonquin Regiment (likely a scout car equipped with a radio) was moved to the corner of the Dwarsdijk and the Boomdijk, on the farm of the Koolen family [1].

Sector Groenedijk/Welbergsedijk

Given the relative success of "D" Coy on the Welbergsedijk, "C" Coy (led by Major Herbert) was moved up in the direction of the Welbergsedijk to exploit the advance. They advanced via Kromwielswegje to reach Welberg from behind (Q15). "C" Coy's objective was sector "Keith" (Laurentiusdijk to Kromwielswegje). To reinforce the anti-tank defences, the troop of self-propelled anti-tank guns that had been kept in reserve ("C" Troop, 96 Battery, 5th Anti-Tank Regiment RCA) was added to the main force under cover of a smoke screen. The group of M-10's positioned itself in a defensive formation as well as they could in the dark, to deal with a possible tank attack. They were deployed in the backyards of the houses between Kromwielswegje and the Groenedijk (P12). Lieutenant Hooke, the troop commander, went around on foot, under fire, to make sure the vehicles were set up in the most effective defensive position. At dawn, these preparations paid off. The Germans attacked from the direction of the water tower with an infantry platoon supported by a Tiger tank[13] and two SPGs. The German attackers were clearly unaware of the exact location of the Algonquins and could be heard talking and shouting as they approached. The crews of the waiting anti-tank guns were quickly

---

[13] The sources consulted ([36], [45], and [49]) do mention a Tiger tank. Officially, the German units in Welberg were not equipped with Tiger tanks, but there may have been a stray Tiger tank present, or a different type of German tank, or (more likely) a self-propelled assault gun. The latter assumption would imply, however, that a number of primary sources were incorrect. Since it has not been possible to confirm the nature of the vehicle in question, it will be referred to as a "Tiger tank."

alerted, and a group of infantrymen, led by Sergeant George Campbell, were equipped with additional PIATs and ammunition to destroy the attacking tanks. As soon as the tanks reached the Welbergsedijk (near Kromwielswegje), the PIAT team struck ... and missed. The Germans instantly returned fire with all the weapons at their disposal. The Algonquins withdrew about a hundred metres and took cover in the cellars of the houses lining the road. This meant that Lieutenant Hooke's M-10 troop was left without infantry support. Fortunately, their position was out of the direct line of sight of the enemy tanks. Also, a troop of tanks from the South Alberta Regiment had arrived behind the Welbergsedijk at dawn and the troop commander volunteered to sweep the road in his Sherman and join battle with the Tiger. This would have been an unequal fight since the Tiger tank completely outclassed the Sherman in terms of both armament and armour plating. In addition, the road was a winding one and the Tiger would be in a fire position to knock out the first tank that came around the corner (Cassidy 196).

"D" COMPANY RIGHT-HOOK INTO WELBERG (SECOND BATTLE)

Drawing by Major Cassidy. From Warpath, *the regimental history of the Algonquin Regiment. Coincidentally, the drawing was made a the same position where the monument stands today [1]*

In his memoirs entitled *Peewees on Parade*, John Galipeau describes an episode that took place at about that time or shortly afterwards. Galipeau was a Private in "A" Squadron of the South Alberta Regiment:

> After travelling two or three hours [from Bergen op Zoom] with little opposition, we arrived at a village where the infantry was attacking and meeting stiff opposition. Sergeant Gove, who was taking charge of the troop temporarily, caught up on us in a tank mounted with a 75 mm gun. He came up to my tank on foot, called me out onto the ground and told me there was a report that a Tiger Tank was concealed behind a barn we could see a quarter of a mile out, sitting by itself in an open field. He wanted me to take it

out with the seventeen-pounder on my tank. I wasn't happy. I figured that if there was a Tiger tank sitting behind that barn, he could see me sooner than I could see him, and any kind of frontal attack was going to be suicide.

As Sergeant Gove and I discussed the best way to handle the alleged Tiger, the decision was taken away from us. There was a double explosion as two rounds of high-explosive shells from an 88 landed nearby moments apart. We were standing beside a building with a heavy dirt roof, well constructed, but only five or six feet high. It looked like it might have been built as a bomb shelter. The only entrance to the building was an opening about two and a half feet square, and the two of us went through that opening at once.

We forgot about going after the Tiger. [46]

Galipeau's troop commander was delivered by scout car a short time later. He had been so drunk the day before that he had been placed under open arrest. Galipeau's tank did not see further action that day [*ibid.*].

Major Cassidy realized that the German defenders had to be confronted in an unconventional manner. He knew that every vehicle and every person that came within sight of the Tiger would immediately come under fire. In view of the superior armament and armour plating of the German vehicle, the outcome of the encounter was predictable. In short, he did not have the means at that point to put the tank out of action in a direct confrontation.

The Tiger, meanwhile, opened fire on company headquarters and the houses behind Welberg and the Groenedijk with high-explosive and anti-tank shells, as described by Private Galipeau.

Civilian fatalities on the Groenedijk

At about this time, a group of close to fifty Welberg residents, travelling on foot, had reached a spot some ten metres from the intersection of the Groenedijk and the Dwarsdijk roads (P12, Map III). The German counter-attack and the artillery salvos caused a number of casualties among this group. Truusje Somers (14 years old) was hit by a shell fragment and died of her injuries on 5 November in the hospital of Bergen op Zoom. Cornelius de Jong (34) was en route with his whole family when a shell fragment separated his head from his torso. The child he was carrying in his arms was unhurt. Petrus Geers (57) was also fatally injured. Among the wounded were Mrs Gorissen, who would henceforth go through life with a wooden leg, and Mrs Beleter, who was hit in the buttock. Mrs Mijntje Baartmans-Bastiaansen sustained a minor injury to her shoulder.

Janus Geers was a witness to the above tragedy. On 1 November, the Germans had evicted both him and his family and the Gelten family from their shelter. Together with around fifty other Welberg residents, they had taken refuge in farmer Bogers' barn on the corner of the Welbergsedijk and the Groenedijk (P12, Map III). The bombing raid on

Petrus Geers. Killed by artillery fire on the Groenedijk road (collection P. Adriaansen).

63

2 November caused extreme panic among the group. The noise was ear-shattering and the ground shook with every impact. As in many other places in Welberg that day, the desperate residents never stopped praying. One bomb exploded with a great roar on the Groenedijk, only a few dozen metres from the barn, and its occupants decided not to wait inside for the next hit. They fled northwards, in the direction of the Afgeslechtedijk (P10, Map III). A hundred metres into the polder, they took refuge in a ditch, huddling together for warmth. It was very cold and wet, and everyone grew chilled to the bone. Towards morning, the battle noise diminished and the occupants of the ditch believed the fight to be over. Profoundly relieved, they crawled out of the ditch and headed back to the Welbergsedijk. At the end of the Welbergsedijk and along the Groenedijk, the road was packed with Canadian vehicles (the tanks of the South Albertas and the carriers of the Algonquin Regiment). There was not a soul to be seen at that moment. Then the hatch cover of one of the tanks popped open and a crew member urgently waved them into cover. The Canadian evidently knew that the Germans were on their way to launch a counter-attack. The group rushed off towards the Dwarsdijk, but fate struck just before they reached the junction. As described on p. 63, several people were killed and a number wounded. Mrs Snoeijers, who lived at the end of the Groenedijk, remembers 32 wounded being treated in the farmhouse kitchen. The survivors ran on in blind panic towards the polder drainage canal. Canadian ambulances arrived in short order to collect the wounded civilians as well as a number of injured Canadians. The ambulances returned to Moerstraten via the Dwarsdijk and the Boomdijk.

Piet Geers sustained only a minor injury, a scrape to his finger. Years earlier, he had lost the tip of that finger and the superficial wound was oozing blood from what remained of the digit. In the panic that reigned, the injury was misjudged and he was transported to Bergen op Zoom and on to Antwerp, together with seriously injured residents of Welberg. When it was determined that his injury was minor, he was immediately dismissed from the hospital, and he found himself forced to set out on foot for the long journey back to Welberg.

Bart Gorissen and his family, who had fled back to the communal shelter from their house on the Welbergsedijk, were evicted from the shelter not long after that. Two soldiers entered, yelling "Raus" (out). Five German soldiers took the place of the frightened Welberg residents, who fled to farmer Adriaansen's barn, together with the Veraart family. The barn already sheltered a number of residents, sitting on the straw. Then the barn was hit by two consecutive shells and caught fire, forcing the Gorissens to flee once more. Since no one had any idea of where they might find safety, the family joined a large group of people (Jan Ligtenberg among them) heading into the polder, towards De Weel. Travelling along a ditch in the fields, they met up with more Welberg residents, including the Geers family (see above) and took part in a discussion about the best course of action. Conditions in the ditch being far from comfortable, one group decided to flee towards the polder drainage canal. They safely crossed the canal but when they reached the Wijnen farm, they were ordered back by half a dozen Germans and the whole group returned to the ditch. Later that night, Arjan Gorissen spotted five people crossing the ditch and disappearing in the direction of the water tower. These may have been the Germans who had occupied the farm of the Wijnen family. At that point, Jan Huijgen and Arjan Gorissen set out to reconnoitre the polder drainage canal and returned a short time later to fetch the rest of the group, reporting that the Germans had disappeared. Bart Gorissen and his family finally managed to reach safety that morning. The Gorissens and other Welberg residents safely arrived at the Huismans farm, where they were given sandwiches and coffee.

Tinus Gorissen and Kees van Rooi, who had been wounded, were taken to Antwerp by the Canadians. They returned the next day, their injuries treated and bandaged.

Kees van Eekelen, who had fled from Wipstraat to the barn owned by Rikus van Terheijden on the Welbergsedijk, remembers several episodes. After the Canadians captured objective "Scotty" north of Welberg (see Map VII, p. 54), the people in Welberg told them that a German officer was hiding in the loft of a barn. The German had evidently had enough of the war. He ignored repeated commands to come down and stayed where he was. Eventually, Mr Suijkerbuijk gathered his courage and mounted the steps to the attic, equipped with a flashlight and followed by an armed Canadian. They finally convinced the German *Feldwebel* (sergeant) to descend, and the Canadians quickly relieved him of his decorations and epaulets. The *Feldwebel* ended his inglorious career in captivity.

Two photos showing Steenbergen residents and men of the 5th Anti-Tank Regiment RCA. The exact location is unknown (collection P. Adriaansen).

When the Canadians were forced to retreat several hundred metres, Kees van Eekelen and his family, along with some of the other refugees from the Terheijden barn, fled to the Groenedijk. At one point, he took shelter behind the lifeless body of Kees de Jong on the east side of the Groenedijk to protect himself against the exploding shells. Both Canadian and civilian wounded were lying along the outside of the dike. The group, fleeing along the safe side of the dike, made its way to the crossing over the Polderwatergang (P11). There, Henk Augustijn was waiting to ferry people across in a small boat, since the Germans had blown up the bridge. Once across, people spotted a sign saying "Verges checked to 8 feet" and saw white cotton ribbons by the side of the road. They realized that they were lucky that nobody had stepped on a mine. Evidently, the mine-clearing sections of the Canadian Engineers had checked the Groenedijk as far as the Watergang canal but not in the direction of Welberg[14].

In the course of the fighting near the Welbergsedijk, Janus Helmons was injured by a Canadian hand grenade that exploded in his shelter.

---

[14] A section of 8 Field Squadron RCE, led by Lieutenant Lake, started clearing mines on the Groenedijk on 2 November at 2140 hrs [43].

The advance to the Cornelius church

Back on the Welbergsedijk, "D" Coy still faced the problem of the Tiger tank and a German SPG stationed behind the near-by barn of the Pietershof farm (owned by the Adriaansen

Capt. Dossett
*Lt. Baillargeon
Capt. Carberry
Maj. Warwick
*Lt. Henderson
*Lt. Riches
Lt. Hooke
—At CAEN.

* Killed in action.

Image from the regimental history of the 5th Anti-Tank Regiment RCA. Lieutenant Hooke is pictured on the right, wearing a helmet [10].

family). "D" Coy had not yet come up with an effective plan to put them out of action. The Canadian SPGs were not in a good position to destroy the enemy tanks, and advancing

Sergeant H. A. Honey, 5th Anti-Tank Regiment RCA. He was killed shortly after he destroyed a tank on the Welbergsedijk (photo Edmonton Journal)

dismounted against the German tanks would end in catastrophe as the attacking Algonquins would be decimated by the German infantry covering the tanks. Sergeant Jimmy Lafontaine volunteered to reconnoitre a position to which the 6-pounder anti-tank gun could be manhandled. He found an ideal position behind a board fence from where they could take aim at the enemy monsters unseen. Unfortunately, the gun's crew was spotted as they made their way towards the position they had chosen. The Germans immediately opened fire and the chance was lost [Cassidy 196].

Finally, Major Cassidy, the company commander in charge of the action, decided to employ artillery. He requested a medium artillery regiment to shell the positions of the German tanks on the Welbergsedijk. It was a risky decision, since the German tanks were located at a distance of no more than 100 to 200 metres away from his own troops. The artillery asked him to acknowledge that he accepted responsibility for the action (this was the rule, given the high risk of casualties from friendly fire) and he ordered his men "to dig deep in their slits and cellars and hang on" (Cassidy 197). A few minutes later, a nice, tight concentration of shells fell exactly on target (*ibid.*).

Meanwhile, as Major Cassidy was bringing in the artillery, Sergeant Honey (96th Battery, 5th Anti-Tank Regiment RCA commanded by Lieutenant Hooke) decided to try and get a shot at the armoured vehicles. He started to manoeuvre his SPG to a more favourable position, only to have it bottom out crossing a deep ditch. Sergeant Honey dismounted from his vehicle to inspect the situation and determine whether it was possible to take action from his current position. The German SPG was moved a few metres when the artillery shells requested by Major Cassidy started falling and was now sitting behind a barn. This was a development that significantly improved Sergeant Honey's chances. To his experienced eye, it was clear that if he fired right through the barn, he had a good chance of hitting the SPG. He aimed his 17-pounder gun and gave the order to fire. The massive shell flew right through the barn as planned, passed several houses, and hit the intended target. The German gun exploded and burned like a torch. The crew of the Tiger evidently decided that the situation was getting too hot for comfort and turned tail, fleeing back towards Steenbergen. Sergeant Honey and the other anti-tank gunners sprayed the departing Germans with their heavy .50 Browning machine guns. The German infantry, now without armoured support, lost their nerve and "broke as one man and streaked down the street, dashing behind and through buildings as they went," fleeing along the Welbergsedijk towards the Laurentiusdijk in the direction of Steenbergen [Cassidy 197, Claxton].

Larry Brown, who served as a Private with 15 Platoon, "C" Coy, the Algonquin Regiment, describes the situation with the German tank in his book *Those Army Days*:

Nick Boyko in England, 1945 (photo L. Brown).

We were ready to attack at dawn. It had been a long cold night and every time we stopped, we had to dig in. I remember Nick and I had dug seven slit trenches that night. We would just get one finished and then we would move on. At dawn, we started into the village in utter silence, no firing, no talking. The "Jerries" didn't know we were there behind them until the firing started. It was quiet at our end of the village and we thought maybe the "Jerries" had moved out. Cpl. Allemang was leading our section, Conrad was next and then me. A sniper shot Allemang in the chest. Conrad and I got him into the ditch, but he was gone. We stayed in the ditch until the tanks started firing, then we started to go through an orchard with a ditch along one side and a hedge on the other side of the ditch. There was an opening in the hedge, so we went through it towards a barn about 150 feet away. There was a German Tiger tank sitting by the corner of the barn. Its turret and big gun was slowly turning toward us. We lost no time going back through that hedge and into the ditch. The Tiger fired and the shell went through the hedge over our heads. We were deafened for a few moments. But, one of our tanks had spotted the Tiger and let blast at it. That Tiger was out of action and the "Jerries" started running to get away. Cpl. Dave Pierce nabbed one of them and stripped him of his weapons. He gave the Luger to Foster, a new fellow who had just joined us four days before. He had been in the Signal Corps and wanted to see more action, so transferred to us. Later, when it quieted down, we dug our slit trenches and stayed put in the orchard. We were waiting for further orders. I was getting my 40 winks while Nick stood guard. Nick woke me up to tell me George Phillips had been hit in the next slit trench. I thought he had been hit by a sniper, but it had been an 88 fired from a tank. It hit him on the left side at his waist and took half his stomach out. We tried to put field dressings on him but he would rip them off as fast as we put them on. He lived about fifteen minutes and then he was gone. We sure missed him, as he was a good fellow to be with and he was quite popular with everyone. A few minutes later another 88 hit Foster and he was gone also. It sure made the rest of us very nervous and wondering who would be next. Fortunately, our tanks had started firing back and the "Jerry" tank cleared out The 88 was one of the most feared guns on a tank. They could pick off our guys as good as a sniper. We lost three guys out of our platoon that day. Foster's newly acquired Luger was found lodged in a tree trunk with the barrel bent and his gear hanging in shreds. The shell had gone through him and exploded in the tree behind him. I guess he never knew what hit him. He had only been with us four days. He didn't see very much action. Our Coy was relieved by another and we were taken out for a rest. The Germans had retreated to the next town of Steenbergen. [49]

Thanks to the personal initiative and skills of Lieutenant Hooke and Sergeant Honey, the situation facing the Canadians had significantly improved. The 21-year old sergeant from Dewberry, AB, received a Mention in Dispatches for his actions.[15] Sadly, he was killed a short time later in his M-10 by a long-range shot fired by the same Tiger tank that had fled earlier. Private E.H. Riley lost his life in the same incident, but the rest of the crew escaped unhurt. Lieutenant J.C. Hooke was awarded a Military Cross for his part in destroying the German SPG.

The South Alberta tanks advanced with the men of "C" Coy of the Algonquin Regiment. They reached the church around noon, approaching via Corneliusstraat (H9, Map IV). Major Cassidy followed their progress over the radio. The (unidentified) troop leader of the South Albertas had been wounded and one of the corporals had taken over command of the troop. Unfamiliar with this new role, the corporal voiced a series of complaints that could be heard by everyone on the radio net. Everything was very confused, he said, and he was out of ammunition; there were an awful lot of Jerries running around, what the hell was it all about anyway, and what the hell was he doing there, would someone please tell him?

Uniform of an unidentified Sergeant of the 5th Anti-Tank Regiment (collection of the author).

---

[15] A small body of water near Lac La Biche in Alberta was renamed in Sergeant Honey's honour. Lake Honey was dedicated to Lance Sergeant Hedley Arthur Honey on September 15, 2007. The name was bestowed by the Canadian Permanent Committee on Geographical Names (now the Geographical Names Board of Canada). The Memorial Cairns Project was conducted by the Airman's Memorial Cairns Committee, Royal Canadian Legion, McGrane Branch No 28, Lac La Biche, Alberta.

Fortunately, the chaos was not as bad as he made out and this battle ended a short time later. Welberg was finally free (Cassidy 198).

The war in Welberg was not yet over, however. A group of Germans in the woods near the Eekelenberg farm remained under fire from the heavy mortars of the New Brunswick Rangers and the artillery in Halsteren. The Germans, in turn, directed artillery fire at both Welberg and the Boomdijk. The shelling continued for the rest of the day. In retrospect, the German artillery fire heralded the total withdrawal of the Germans from West Brabant.

The artillery fire interfered with the attempt of the Argyll and Sutherland Highlanders of Canada to reach Welberg via the Boomdijk/Wipstraat roads. The vehicles of this battalion were massed on the Boomdijk road halfway to Moerstraten, waiting for the signal to advance to Steenbergen. The German fire caused several casualties when two carriers of the Algonquins were hit. One soldier was killed and one wounded.

One of the shells exploded in the midst of a section of men from "D" Coy, Algonquin Regiment, who had gathered for a meal in a house in Welberg. All members of the section were either killed or wounded. Given the fact that "D" Coy had lost not a single man during the battles with the Germans, this proved to be a particularly bitter and tragic event.

Another Canadian soldier lost his life at the intersection of the Boomdijk and the Dwarsdijk. His body hung upside down in a ditch, underneath his motorcycle. Dozens of Canadians spent time in the barn on the Koolens' farm that day, and the single kitbag that remained behind the next day no doubt belonged to the victim in the ditch. It was stencilled with the name "L.P. Smith."[16]

Private Gordon Taylor (author's collection)

Sector Oudlandsestraat

The attack on the evening of 2 November was launched from the tank wall on Oudlandsestraat, simultaneous with the attack of the Algonquins. As described, the Lincoln and Welland Regiment had been unable to break through the German defence.

Private Gordon Taylor of "D" Coy, Lincoln and Welland Regiment, distinguished himself during the night of 2/3 November. Aware that the company's fighting strength was critically low, he continued to man his machine gun throughout the night in spite of a serious wound to his leg. It was not until the following morning that he finally agreed to go back for medical treatment, but only after receiving a direct order from his platoon commander. He nearly lost his leg as a result [29]. He was awarded the Military Medal for his actions.

At 0350 hrs, the commander of "D" Coy, Captain R.F. Dickie, ordered the SPGs of the 14th Rainbow Battery to advance. The German SPG shelling "D" Coy at the Panhoef farm, probably from a position on Oudlandsdijkje, had to be put out of action. At 1000 hrs, two SPGs

---

[16] Private Lorne Paisley Smith lies buried in the War Cemetery in Bergen op Zoom.

from "K" Troop (14 Battery, 5th Anti-Tank Regiment RCA) were destroyed at their advance positions near the Panhoef farm on Oudlandsestraat (N15). The artillery unit suffered seven casualties, of which five were fatal. Bombardier D.E. Obre and Gunners H.B. Gunnarsen, C.J. Horner, N. Rodgers, and S. Scott were killed, and Sergeant J.A. Wright and Gunner T.S. Rompf were wounded by shell fragments [10, 43].

Ultimately, the honour of destroying the German SPG was claimed by the artillery. The FOO of the 15th Field Regiment RCA (Captain Griffin) reported that his group had dismounted from their vehicle. Private Ferguson carried the heavy radio on his back as Captain Griffin coordinated the fire. The aim was perfect, and the German SPG was put out of action [12].

Once the German gun had been disabled, the situation became less intense. Reconnaissance patrols were sent out from both the tank wall and the position of "D" Coy to explore the German defence. The patrols located several German positions. Once these were rolled up, "D", "A", and "C" Coys finally managed to advance.

At 1020 hrs, a patrol was ordered to the corner of Koolbaantje and Bergse Grintweg (D10, Map IV). A lone scout sent ahead by the patrol reached the houses on Koolbaantje and took a German prisoner, who told him about the strength of the defence in the area. The men defending the sector belonged to 10 Coy, 6th *Fallschirmjäger* Regiment.

The Germans spotted the patrol soon afterwards and machine gun fire from the hamlet of Waterhoefke forced the men to retreat. It was clear that the Germans were not yet ready to give up.

While the heavy Vickers machine guns of the New Brunswick Rangers were directing fire at the sector north of the Canadian positions, "C" Coy of the Lincoln and Welland Regiment made contact with the Algonquins on Hoog-straat, within the built-up area of Welberg. This took place at 1715 hrs. Meanwhile, the German defensive line on the right flank (Welberg) had been rolled up.

In spite of the success on the right flank, however, resistance on the left flank remained strong. German

An M-10 tank of the 5th Regiment somewhere near Steenbergen. The open turret is covered by an improvised steel plate welded in place. This was common practice, to prevent the enemy from destroying the vehicle by tossing in hand grenades (collection P. Adriaansen).

defensive fire, especially from the positions at Waterhoefke and along Bergse Grintweg and Koolbaantje, was causing delay. At around 2235 hrs that evening, the Lincoln and Welland Regiment finally managed to secure the intersection of Koolbaantje and Bergse Grintweg (E9,

Map IV), in spite of heavy machine gun fire. In the end, "J" Troop of the 5th Anti-Tank Regiment RCA (14 Battery), supported by a squadron of the South Albertas, forced a breakthrough. A number of German defensive positions were destroyed in the course of this action and the resistance on the left flank was finally broken.

Around 2235 hrs, sounds reaching the Canadians indicated that the Germans were in the process of retreating from this forward front sector. A patrol reaching Waterhoefke at 0200 hrs (4 November) reported finding signs of a hasty departure. A candle was found still burning in one of the houses and food was left out on the table. The same patrol also made contact with the Canadian troops on the Halsteren side of the Ligne river.

A second patrol eventually reached Burgemeester van Loonstraat (D7, Map IV), proceeding along Bergse Grintweg. It met no resistance and made contact with a patrol of the Argyll and Sutherland Highlanders of Canada [38, 8, 10].

Ross Munro, the Canadian Press's lead European war correspondent in WWII, published an article on 22 November recounting the adventures of the Lincoln and Welland Regiment. He described the action in Steenbergen as follows:

> In this attack, Lincs fought Goering troops and men of the 6th Parachute Regiment. It was heavy going but the German defence was broken by the Lincs and other Ontario battalions, and a central Ontario unit captured Steenbergen.
>
> A German prisoner captured on this push paid the Lincs a backhanded compliment when he said: "The Lincoln and Welland Regiment has no sentiment, no mercy, no discipline." The Lincs themselves liked that.
>
> It was on the advance to Steenbergen where Capt. Lambert, one of the fabulous characters in the regiment, gave the battalion one of its biggest laughs. Lambert fights a war the way they fight it in the movies. He goes into action without any helmet, his crop of hair waving in the wind. He shouts and yells and encourages his men. In the middle of this fight, he wandered over the battlefield shouting "ice cream, peanuts, chewing gum, ginger ale," as if he was in a ball park. The Germans thought the Lincs were crazy as loons.[17]

Sector Steenbergen

At nightfall, the Argylls were ready to attack Steenbergen. Two troops of the British Fife and Forfar Yeomanry Regiment (part of the 79th British Armoured Division), each equipped with four Crocodiles (Churchill flame-throwing tanks), were added to the Argylls' attack force for extra support. Captain Sinclair, the Forward Observation Officer of the 15th Field Regiment RCA, was responsible for artillery support. The force had moved up to the Boomdijk that afternoon in a long column, at a safe distance from the battle zone. In spite of the distance to the front, the situation was still very hazardous. The German artillery and mortars had zeroed in on the Boomdijk and were delivering accurate fire. The Argylls mention in their regimental history

---

[17] Retrieved from http://collections.civilisations.ca/warclip/objects/common/webmedia.php?irn=5028010. Captain Herbert Owen Lambert was American by birth. He was killed on 26 January 1945 at Kapelseveer. The last time he was seen, he was marching towards the German lines, cursing and swearing, surrounded by smoke. He is buried in Bergen op Zoom.

that it is a miracle they did not suffer any casualties. The advance was held up by a Fife and Forfar Yeomanry Crocodile that became immobilized right across the Boomdijk. To minimize the expected resistance, the advance was preceded by an artillery bombardment on Steenbergen.

The attack plan was put together by the acting commander, Major Stockloser. Three companies would set up an attack position in Welberg. Once in position, "C" Coy would mount a frontal attack on Steenbergen via Wipstraat, with the objective of seizing the intersection of Krommeweg and Molenstraat (F7, Map IV). Depending on the outcome, one of the companies would then advance to the centre of the town. Just before the attack, Major Stockloser and his company commanders became embroiled in a major argument. The promised artillery and tank support had not yet arrived and the company commanders objected to launching the attack without support. The attack finally commenced when the support had been organized [34].

The crew of an M-10 poses for the camera somewhere in Steenbergen. The tank bears the name "JEAN," which makes it part of "J" Troop, 14 Battery (collection J. van Doorn)

The men of "C" Coy reached the intersection of Molenweg and Wipstraat at approximately 0125 hrs (4 November). Strong patrols were sent out towards Bergse Grintweg and the water tower. The patrol to the water tower was given the objective of cordoning off the road in the direction of Dinteloord to block German access. The western patrol had orders to make contact with the Lincoln and Welland Regiment. At 0200 hrs, the Argyll and Sutherland Highlanders of Canada and the Lincoln and Welland Regiment made contact on Burgemeester Van Loonstraat. The main force of the Argylls advanced along Wouwsestraat towards the centre. A short time later, they received a signal from Brigade Headquarters that the centre of Steenbergen had been reached. The enemy had fled, with the exception of a few snipers who claimed two more victims. Captain Jack Prugh (commanding "D" Coy) and Private Ronald

MacPheron died as a result of the well-aimed shots by one of the snipers. Steenbergen was consolidated by early morning [7].

Captain Sam Chapman ("C" Coy, Argyll and Sutherland Highlanders of Canada) describes his experiences in Steenbergen in a letter to his wife dated 5 November 1944:

> We had a bit of a do, but "C" coy had all the best of it except we spent some miserable (from the weather) hours – about 36 –, and waiting to pass through after somebody else has done their job is pretty hard on the nerves. My stomach was in a first class knot till we finally got going and I was visibly shaking from cold + nerves. In any event I have now taken a coy into a show and we actually "captured" a town. We hit just at dawn and all the Jerries except a postal corps fellow + one wounded S.S. had beetled off. As the C.S.M. [SSMM H.T. Sharpe] + I poke our way down the street and one or two very shaken civilians poked their heads out of door[s] and broke into tears at the sight of us, I felt a thrill I've never experienced before. Sometime I'll tell you the name of the place where I took the first coy in. [34, p. 317]

Sector Glymes/ Kladde

As previously mentioned, elements of the South Alberta Regiment, the Argyll and Sutherland Highlanders of Canada, the New Brunswick Rangers, and the 8th Anti-Aircraft Regiment RCA occupied the positions around Halsteren and Lepelstraat. These troops were relieved at approximately 1000 hrs by the British Columbia Regiment and the Lake Superior Regiment. The rest period for the men of the 4th Armoured Brigade near Heerle had been brief. Orders to clear Nieuw-Vossemeer, Heense Molen, and Sint Philipsland of enemy soldiers followed almost immediately. To reconnoitre the German positions near Kladde and Glymes, a patrol consisting of two carriers of the Lake Superior Regiment was sent out from Halsteren shortly after midday. When they reached Lepelstraat (G16), the Canadians asked the local population for volunteers to accompany them as guides. No one volunteered, in the knowledge that the area near Glymes was littered with mines. People also suspected that not all the Germans had left the area. The patrol carried on. At the end of Glymesweg, the front carrier advanced a short distance along the dike. A soldier dismounted, took a quick look around, and immediately jumped back into the carrier. The vehicle reversed to turn around and quickly accelerated to return along the same route. The rapid acceleration caused one of the tracks to hit the verge and the vehicle was instantly blown up by a mine, killing Lieutenant Stark and the driver, Private Hiebert. The other carrier returned towards Lepelstraat without mishap. No enemy activity was reported [31, 13].

Saturday 4 November was a clear, bright day.

The German retreat

As the fighting continued in Welberg, the Germans continued to withdraw both soldiers and supplies. Boats came and went from Dintelsas and Willemstad to Numansdorp and Goeree Overflakkee. Other troops were taken north, via Zijpe. By 4 November, the Germans were in full

88 mm gun barrel near the farm house of the Huijsmans family (collection of the author).

retreat. The decision to withdraw from Steenbergen was probably based less on a direct defeat at the hands of the Canadians than on strategic grounds as by then, the 104th American Infantry Division had broken through the front at the Mark river further to the east. From Standdaarbuiten, they were able to push on towards Klundert, east of Willemstad. The British 49th Division had already reached Fijnaart at that point (east of Dinteloord).

On 5 November, the front of the German 67th Army Corps was split in two parts. Some of the troops were located near Willemstad while the rest were positioned near the access ramp to the Moerdijk bridges. The decision was made to evacuate the western flank and concentrate all energy on keeping the Moerdijk position open as long as possible. These efforts were successful until 9 November, the day that marked the end of the German presence in West Brabant.

Since the main road from Steenbergen to Dinteloord was already under fire, the last troops to leave made their way from Steenbergen and Nieuw-Vossemeer via the Benedensas lock at De Heen (H8) through the Dinteloord polder to Dintelsas (S2). Many others crossed the Volkerak (part of the Rhine–Meuse–Scheldt delta [A-Q2]) to Goeree Overflakkee in flatboats.

A German gun was positioned in the farmyard of the Huijsmans family near Benedensas. Just before the retreat, the gun was blown up and the ammunition trailer set on fire. The barrel of the 88 mm anti-tank gun remained behind on the farm and is still there today, set into the ground next to the barn (see photo above) [26].

Paratrooper Wolfgang Langer described his experiences in a regimental history of the 6th Fallschirmjäger Regiment. The following extract illustrates the situation during the German retreat:

We marched past Steenbergen and moved into a farm near Dinteloord. Steenbergen had become the main battle front and all hell had broken loose there. A continuous stream of fighter-bombers dropped their bombs, setting the small town ablaze from one end to the other. At nightfall, we received orders to retreat to the Dintel locks (Dintel Sas), where they were ferrying the troops across the sea arm to Numansdorp. Dinteloord was also ablaze by now. We moved towards the embarkation point at the Dintel locks. The scene was utter chaos. The embarkation point was under continuous fire from long-barrelled guns, and every time one of the ferry boats pulled in, all hell broke loose again. There were bunkers and trenches where we could take cover, so that the losses, although high, were not as bad as they might have been. I lost several people, including Schmidt. He was a red-headed fellow from Berlin with an irrepressible sense of humour. A shell fragment hit him in the chest and he died instantly. [27]

Langer's section received sudden orders to proceed to Willemstad, north-east of Dintelsas. In the chaos, it was impossible to find all the members of the mortar section, so the depleted group, inadequately armed, set out for the burning town of Dinteloord. They spent several days in Willemstad, where they occupied a position but saw little action. Finally, they were taken across the Hollands Diep in motorboats. They were strafed by aircraft during their crossing, but Langer's boat was lucky and reached its destination unharmed. The others were not so fortunate and drowned in the icy water [27].

Sector Steenbergen

In Steenbergen, the situation was under the complete control of the Argylls. Captain Rathbone, the commander of the mortar platoon, took over command from Captain Prugh, the commander of "D" Coy, who had been killed. They took a number of prisoners that morning (including deserters), half of them paratroopers from the 6th *Fallschirmjäger* Regiment, half of them soldiers of the Hermann Goering Regiment. At 0930 hrs, the Canadian battalion reported that Steenbergen had been consolidated [7].

Canadian vehicles in the market square in early November 1944 [16]

It was the sudden silence that told local residents that the battle was over. One resident remembers that the streets were deserted around 0700 hrs. The first Canadians were spotted at the intersection of Kade and Burgemeester Van Loonstraat (D6, Map IV). The news spread like wildfire and within minutes, the local population swarmed around the liberators. The soldiers, although filthy from battle and looking weary, were very friendly and handed out chocolates and cigarettes. Following the directions of local residents, they took a few more German prisoners, who were found asleep at various locations. The prisoners, hands on their heads, were taken away by the Canadians.

The liberators swiftly tackled the job of clearing debris and in no time, the streets were lined by neatly swept piles of rubble. People immediately began making emergency repairs to their damaged homes. Here and there, a long-hidden Dutch flag was unfurled and hung out. Local resistance members of the O.D. were already in evidence that morning, wearing orange arm bands.

The story is told that a small group of Germans in Heense Molen (F9) was disarmed by resistance fighter Henk van Mechelen from Steenbergen. It was a peaceful scene: the Germans were overjoyed to be able to hand over their weapons. This story is confirmed by Canadian historical records, although the Van Mechelen name is not mentioned. Prior to the arrival of the Lake Superior Regiment, the hamlet of De Heen also received a visit from members of the O.D.

The community spirit of the population was not shared by everyone: some of the evacuees discovered on their return that their possessions had changed ownership—an unpleasant surprise but a phenomenon of all times and all places [51].

In Steenbergen, meanwhile, Canadian engineers were busy clearing the roads of mines and obstacles. Apart from the mines and tank walls, the unpaved roads had been rendered impassable by the deep ruts left by the tanks. The steel behemoths, weighing over 30 tons, had completely torn up the unpaved (dike) roads. Ruts up to half a metre deep made even foot traffic a challenge. The Canadians most probably levelled the main roads while the local residents repaired the secondary roads.

A Canadian bulldozer fills a crater with the front wall of the Aarden Hotel (4 November 1944) [16]

Early in the morning, 3 Troop, 8 Field Squadron RCE, cleared a route past the tank wall on Oudlandseweg of mines. They found four wooden mines, and early in the evening, a bulldozer was destroyed by a mine near the same tank wall. The vehicle wreck remained on the edge of a ditch for several days after the liberation. Four engineers were wounded in the incident.

Four large craters with a diameter of close to ten metres, half filled with water, were filled with rubble. One of the vehicles involved in the clean-up operation was destroyed by a mine. The craters were close together, at the intersection of Kade and Burgemeester van Loonstraat. The Canadian bulldozer used the front wall of the damaged Aarden Hotel to fill in one of the enormous holes while the local population, armed with spades and shovels, stood by to complete the job. One of the other craters was rendered passable by a Bailey bridge named "Ditchburn Bridge," after the section commander in charge of the construction.

No. 2 Troop, 8 Field Squadron RCE, repaired the crossing over the Boomvaart in Bocht. For pavement, they used bundles of steel pipes (ARMCO corrugated piping) covered with rubble and steel planking. The work was completed shortly after midnight on 4 November [16, 40]. At approximately 4 a.m., the engineers moved their headquarters from Halsteren to Steenbergen, near the sugar factory, where they stayed through 8 November.

Sherman tank of No.1 Squadron, The Governor General's Foot Guards at an unidentified farm, 6 November 1944 (Library and Archives Canada, MIKAN no. 3405744)

The access roads in the area around Steenbergen were not overlooked either. As in Steenbergen, the work consisted primarily of clearing the roads and verges of mines and removing barriers and obstacles. Engineer patrols were sent out toward St. Phillipsland (8 Field Squadron RCE) and Dinteloord (9 Field Squadron RCE). According to the author of *Green Route Up* [16], Lieutenant Brady lost his driver when their vehicle hit a mine northwest of Steenbergen. The driver's name did not feature on the official casualty list, however, so he may have survived his serious injuries. The 15th Field Regiment RCA moved to Halsteren to a position just below Steenbergen. Once again, the soggy ground made it difficult to find a suitable position. For want of a better solution, the guns were placed on the pavement. A gun carrier became so immovably stuck that the steel cable that had been rolled out around a house pulled down the house instead of winching the vehicle out of the mud.

With the British presence in the vicinity of Willemstad and the unclear situation at the front, many no-firing zones were in effect. The soldiers were happy to be able to spend the night in reasonably comfortable circumstances in some of the houses [12].

The South Albertas also moved to Steenbergen, where they were to spend a few days to conduct maintenance and repairs [35].

Returning to Koolbaantje

The Helmons family had fled to Notendaal after several brutal nights in their shelter. Then two Germans on a motorcycle with sidecar plundered their few possessions. What saved the day was that when the thieves fled, they overturned their motor cycle, sidecar and all. They picked themselves up and slunk off amid uproarious laughter from the bystanders. Meanwhile, one of the Helmons returned to the house to fetch the "pig in the barrel" that had been left behind in the consternation (see p. 23). The increased shelling forced him to make his way through ditches. Shells had been hitting Notendaal at irregular intervals, exploding in the flooded polder, but no major damage had been done although several people were injured. Toon Laanen went out to fetch some straw and lived to regret it: an errant shell fragment ripped off his arm. Mrs Backx from Kladde sat down by her window to do some sewing and was suddenly hit in the chest by a shell fragment. She died of her injuries.

A platoon of Canadian soldiers of the Algonquin Regiment on Groeneweg East in Steenbergen. The photo was taken on 4 November 1944 by Mrs Leautaud-van den Bergh (author's collection).

On 4 November, peace descended on the region and the occupants of Koolbaantje returned home. On Kade (D6, Map IV) they encountered their first Canadians, who were just bulldozing the front wall of the Aarden Hotel into the enormous crater described above. Hearing the rumbling of artillery, one of the Helmons sons, who spoke a little English, asked a Canadian officer if the battle was heating up again. Standing in the doorway of a house near the harbour, the officer reassured the boy. "Canadian gunfire," he said. (Given the hour, the artillery fire heard was probably in support of the attack across the Steenbergse Vliet.)

When the Helmons arrived at their home address on Koolbaantje, they found a chaos that exceeded their worst fears. Both the house and the barn had been reduced to rubble. The many craters and the deep ruts left behind by the tanks made it hazardous to even set foot on the property. Unexploded bomb shells littering the ground had to be carefully circumnavigated. The field in front of the house (measuring approximately 50 x 50 metres) had been transformed into a moonscape dotted with at least 25 craters. The cat had put on considerable weight after consuming the rabbits and chickens that had been killed in the fighting. The chicken coop itself was reduced to a pile of reddish, feather-strewn rubble. The goat was still alive, although his back seemed alarmingly red. Fortunately, this proved to be the result of brick dust raining down on the unsuspecting animal.

Tragedy strikes the Van Hooijdonk and Van de Oudera families

Riet van Hooijdonk lived on Kinderbaantje (J9, Map IV). The youngest in a large family, she had barely been touched by the war—if anything, it had seemed like a carefree adventure. But that all changed the day the war came to Welberg. Unlike the preceding years, her experiences in the midst of battle would leave a deep and indelible impression on the then 14-year old girl.

In the early days of November 1944, a German SPG cautiously rolled along Kinderbaantje and took up position at the end of the road to shell the Canadians on the Boomdijk and Canadezenweg - an action being repeated all over Welberg. The gun blasts whipped up grey clouds of dust between the houses on Kinderbaantje and doors rattled in their frames, shaken by the thundering explosions. The Canadians wasted no time in responding and opened fire on the German tank. One of their shells hit the home-made shelter in the backyard where Riet and her family were hiding from the war violence. Fortunately, no one was hurt, but the situation had become so alarming that Riet's father, Jan van Hooijdonk, decided to move his family to safety, away from the inferno.

Moving east along the Welbergsedijk road and then turning south, the family fled towards the home of one of Riet's older sisters, who lived in 't Werfke (a housing development on Kromwielswegje near the Welbergsedijk road). They reached their destination without mishaps, only to discover that the situation there was just as dangerous. They could hear the barking of a German machine-gun concealed in the brush, spewing its deadly load at the Canadian position. The Canadians delivered counter fire and bullets whizzed by and landed in the immediate vicinity. Van Hooijdonk had brought along a slaughtered pig in a wheel barrow and when he pushed his precious load into the safety of the barn, he was badly shaken by a volley of bullets that hit the boards of the barn right beside his head. Wood splinters rained down on him and he wisely decided to move on and lead his family out of the danger zone.

They made their way to the "Pietershof" farm, owned by the Adriaansens. Finding the cellar under the farm house already filled to overflowing with terrified Welberg residents, they headed for the shelter that had been dug behind the barn, near the farm house. There were eleven of them: Riet (the narrator of this story), Jan van Hooijdonk (61) and his wife, Riet's sister and her husband Piet Gelten and their two children, Jan van de Ouderaa (68) and his wife Jaan van Hooijdonk (Jan's sister), and their son Bep van de Ouderaa with his fiancé Mies Bokelaar. In the dark shelter, Riet huddled next to her sister, her mother, and her brother-in-law Piet Gelten, as far away as possible from the shelter's entrance. Bep, Jan van Hooijdonk and Jan van de Ouderaa sat across from them, facing the entrance of the shelter. No one spoke, but their sweaty faces, covered in dirt, betrayed their tension.

Without warning, tragedy struck the shelter. An enormous blast made Riet's ears ring and, as if in a dream, she saw Bep van de Ouderaa lying on his side. "Mies, I'm finished," he whispered. His last word before he died of his injuries were: "I see angels coming. Oh no, they are turning away ..." Riet's sister, in a matter-of-fact voice, announced that their father, Jan van Hooijdonk, was dead. Jan van de Ouderaa, who had been closest to the entrance, had taken the full blast of the projectile exploding immediately in front of the entrance. His body was so badly mutilated that he must have died instantly from the effects of the explosion. Riet herself was hit by a shell fragment that penetrated her right ankle. Her left ankle, also hit by a fragment, was swelling up like a balloon but the skin was unbroken.

Bep van de Ouderaa

Piet Gelten urged the others to stay in the shelter rather than flee, fearing that they might be mistaken for soldiers. At that point, footsteps or other sounds must have been heard near the shelter, since all the survivors started shouting: *Hollanders, Hollanders!*, in a desperate attempt to reveal their presence and let the soldiers know that they were civilians. Soon afterwards, Piet Gelten noticed that the straw in the shelter's roof had caught fire. The cramped space filled with suffocating smoke and despite the danger, they were forced to abandon the shelter. Riet's sister was the first to emerge, still shouting *Hollanders, Hollanders!* and holding one of her children in front of her so the soldiers would see at once that they were civilians. Riet remembers seeing her sister or mother covering her father's body with a cloth before they left the inferno of the shelter.

Riet, unable to walk because of her injuries, was carried by Piet Gelten. When they reached Bosmans' café across the road (on the corner of the Welbergsedijk and Welbergswegje), Piet put Riet down on the ground. The Canadians attacked soon afterwards and she remembers being terrified as she watched them stealthily approach, their faces blackened, their helmets camouflaged with branches, their bayonets fixed for hand-to-hand combat. Fortunately, the liberators quickly ascertained that Riet did not pose any danger and transported her and several other civilians to the beer cellar of Bosmans' café. Once in the cellar, she was attended by a doctor wearing a Canadian uniform who proved to be Dutch. Riet remembers that his name was Dr Krijger, and that he told her he was a cousin of Mr Goossens, who lived near the water tower. No further details were known at the time of writing.

That night, probably the night of 2/3 November, they remained in the beer cellar of Bosmans Café, guarded by a big, black Canadian soldier.[18] He sat perched on the stairs leading down into the cellar and in the flickering light of a candle, Riet watched him with fascination. He was the first black person she had ever seen.

---

[18] Unlike the American army, the Canadian army did not discriminate based on race or ethnic origin. Whereas black soldiers in the US were not allowed to serve at the front, black and native Canadians did serve in the front lines, side by side with their Caucasian comrades. It may be noted that since Canada had not known slavery, the black population in Canada was very small at that time. The only black community of any size at that time was in Halifax, Nova Scotia.

The next morning, the civilians were moved from the beer cellar to farmer Bogers' barn (at the corner of the Welbergsedijk and the Groenedijk), where Canadian medics placed Riet on a stretcher and put her in an ambulance, together with three wounded Canadians. Meanwhile, her older brother Piet van Hooijdonk, who lived on Blauwstraat, had learned of the tragedy that had befallen his family, probably alerted by other refugees. He set out for Welberg at once to try and locate his family. Watching through the window of the ambulance, Riet saw him arrive. Her relief quickly turned to despair when the ambulance took off. She saw her brother running after the ambulance, trying to keep up, and then watched him grow smaller and smaller in the distance.

The trip took a long time and Riet suspected, correctly, that they were headed for the hospital in Antwerp. When she arrived there, it soon became obvious that she was not a soldier. Generously provided with white bread and chocolate, she was transported to the civilian hospital in Bergen op Zoom, 50 km away. Filled to overflowing with civilian casualties, the hospital was a madhouse. Every bed was occupied and patients thronged the hallways and stairwells. The staff had their hands full trying to provide even minimal care for all their charges. The bed next to Riet was occupied by a girl whose head was covered in bandages. Not until after the nurse told her that the girl came from Welberg did Riet recognize her as Truusje Somers. The nurse asked her if she knew whether Truusje was Protestant or Catholic. Her condition was so critical that a priest was giving her the last rites. Soon after that, Truusje Somers died of her injuries.

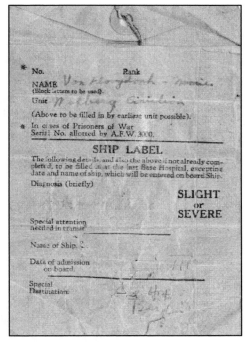

Canadian casualty tag assigned to Mrs van Hooijdonk (collection Mrs van Hooijdonk)

Riet remembers her stay in the hospital as a wretched time. Her father had died and she had no idea whether her mother was still alive, nor did she know the whereabouts of the rest of her family. She was very lonely and cried for hours, overcome by distress. To her horror, doctors standing around her bed discussed the idea of amputating her foot, a fate that fortunately did not come to pass. The shell fragment was removed from her ankle and despite a permanent scar, the injury caused her little trouble in later life.

An explanation of the tragedy was soon in circulation: a notorious collaborator who lived in the neighbourhood and bore the Van Hooijdonks ill will (as evidenced by previous verbal threats) had thrown a hand grenade into the shelter or had caused a German soldier to do so. The story cannot be verified. According to a Canadian source, the Germans who were captured that day had to be protected from the wrath of the Welberg residents.

The Algonquins spent most of that day enjoying some well-deserved rest in Welberg. They made contact with the residents and were told that the curate had been murdered and that a German had thrown a grenade into a shelter, killing its occupants. The latter story no doubt refers to the tragedy above.

That evening (4 November) was the first time the men were able to enjoy a normal meal. They had not seen any food since the night of 2 November. Although a few unlucky ones had guard duty that evening, nearly everyone was able to get a decent night's rest in a dry spot.

The Algonquin carrier platoon was not so lucky. They drove their vehicles in a north-westerly direction towards the Steenbergse Vliet river (P9). Just after midday, they reached the flax factory and reported that the bridge across the Vliet was partly destroyed but passable on foot. The brigade decided to exploit this opportunity and hastily moved up artillery guns as well as the New Brunswick Rangers' machineguns and mortars to reinforce the Algonquins. The engineers were notified that they would have to build a Bailey bridge across the Vliet.

A factory tower (probably that of the flax factory) was used as an observation platform to direct the fire, and "C" and "D" Coys of the Algonquins were selected to secure the far bank of the crossing. The less than enthusiastic soldiers were collected in Welberg and transported towards the bridge. The companies assembled in front of the factory, out of sight of the bridge, and launched the attack an hour and a half after they left Welberg. Artillery fire erupted and the attack unfolded in textbook fashion. The machineguns hurled their lethal loads across the water and smoke bombs and high-explosive shells exploded behind the bridge. "D" Coy was first across the bridge and spread out in the polder. Fortunately for the infantry, they found that the enemy had already left. No. 3 Troop, 9th Field Squadron, immediately started work on a Bailey bridge (2 x 60'DS) [1].

Bailey bridge near the water tower. The bridge was erected by the 9th Field Squadron and bears the name "MacQuarrie" (collection P. Adriaansen).

The two companies stayed behind the bridge on the Dinteloord side that evening. Late at night, two scouts of the Algonquins made contact with the British of the Polar Bear Division, who were in the midst of an attack on Dinteloord. The contact took place a short distance to the east of the main road to Dinteloord. The encounter, unfortunately, resulted in the Algonquins coming under fire from the British. Soldiers of the 11th Battalion Royal Scots Fusiliers threw a hand grenade and fired their rifles before the Canadians were able to identify themselves. Two Algonquin scouts suffered minor injuries (Corporal Neable and Private Turner).

Sector Glymes/Kladde/Nieuw-Vossemeer

The Germans had retreated from this section of the front as well. A patrol from "A" Coy, Lake Superior Regiment, reached Zilverhoekje (east of Steenbergen). The patrol, preceded by two men on foot looking for mines on the road and the verge, made slow progress. This explains why the first Canadian liberators spotted by the residents of Nieuw-Vossemeer were on foot. The men, led by Captain Burke, received a hero's welcome as they entered the town. Among the group were Lieutenant Hinton, CSM Reid, and Privates Bird and Weston. In 1947, a plaque was unveiled on the town hall to commemorate the event, and a neighbouring square was renamed "Burkeplein" (Burke Square). New patrols were sent out from Nieuw-Vossemeer to St Phillipsland, but not a single enemy was spotted. Members of the same regiment also visited Heense Molen and De Heen that day [13].

The ruins of the Roman Catholic church in Dinteloord in 1944 (collection C. Slokkers).

Sector Oudlandsestraat/Bergse Grintweg

At 1035 hrs, "C" and "D" Coy of the Lincoln and Welland Regiment moved to new positions near Waterhoefke and Hoogstraat, south of Steenbergen. As had been reported during the night, the enemy positions were unmanned and the abandoned trenches and houses showed signs of a hasty departure. The relieved soldiers had a chance to clean some of the mud off their gear and stop for a rest, which lasted for the remainder of the day. At noon, replacements arrived at the battalion and since the strength of the companies was down to around 30 men each, the new arrivals were immediately put to work [8].

The tragic bombardment of Dinteloord (S4/5)

While the Canadians reconnoitred the route to the Vliet river, the British units of the 49th Division had moved up from Stampersgat in a westerly direction towards Dinteloord. Thus, the town was approached from two sides: the Canadians from the west via the Bloemendijk and the British from the east via the Noordzeedijk.

As described, the main force of the Germans had already fallen back early in the morning and the Allies could have advanced without encountering much resistance. Only a few defenders were left, armed with light artillery, with orders to delay the advance to the Dintel locks.

Sadly, the information that the Germans had disappeared was apparently not passed on to the British and/or Canadian commanders. Although at least one resident of Dinteloord (baker

Hylke de Jong) notified the British just before an air raid was due to commence, the attempt to call it off came too late.

On Saturday morning, a formation of Allied fighter planes carried out an aerial bombardment of Dinteloord, an action code-named XYN4. At 1010 hrs, twenty-four Spitfires appeared over the unfortunate little town. Twenty minutes later, the attack force was joined by 12 Typhoons armed with rockets [42]. Guns going full-blast, the aircraft swooped down on the undefended town and launched their rockets at the houses below. The ear-shattering explosions took the residents by surprise and they fled in panic. The town caught fire and the devastation was immense. Over 40 residents were killed in this unfortunate attack and to add insult to injury, a few German rearguards blew up the water tower and the windmills that same night.

The next morning, 5 November, more planes arrived over Dinteloord. The soldiers who had arrived by then (probably British) managed to warn the planes by firing tracers but regrettably, the half-destroyed town came once more under fire. Artillery shells exploded in the ruins of the already destroyed Catholic church on Kaai [28].

Left: View of the ruins of Havenweg in Dinteloord (collection J. van Doorn)

Right: The remnants of the destroyed water tower in Dinteloord (collection J. van Doorn)

Starting in the late evening of 4 November until the early morning of 5 November, the entire 4th Armoured Division rumbled through Steenbergen along its narrow, unpaved roads. The throbbing engines of the immense column of trucks, ambulances, reconnaissance vehicles, tanks, and armoured vehicles kept the local residents awake [5].

Dinteloord liberated

On the evening of Sunday 5 November, the carrier platoon and scouts of the Argylls advanced towards Dinteloord without meeting opposition. They entered Dinteloord in the early afternoon, via the Stoofdijk (Q4).

The town of Dinteloord did not welcome the Canadians in the manner to which they had become accustomed. In fact, the atmosphere was far from festive and the welcome distinctly cool. Given the circumstances, this was hardly surprising. The little town was a sorry sight. The air reeked of dust and fire; only a handful of people had remained behind, many sporting makeshift bandages covering their wounds. The sight of the town's senseless destruction and the frosty attitude of the population put a damper on the soldiers' mood, and they continued their advance in silence. Their final destination was the Dintel locks (S2), which they reached without incident.

At the Dintel locks, they were greeted by a scene from Dante's *Inferno*. Critically injured Germans lay moaning on stretchers, their bandages red with blood. Despite quick action by the Argylls to treat the unfortunate enemy, many died of their wounds. Dead horses lay scattered across the terrain, their corpses twisted in grotesque shapes. Military gear and a variety of plundered items were strewn across the ground. Sizable hams, barrels of butter, and large rolls of linen lay abandoned here and there, proof that the thieves had not enjoyed their loot for long. A white flag fluttered above the shell craters that dotted the scene. The Argylls took some forty prisoners, all of Russian origin. They were taken away to Steenbergen, running ahead of the Canadian armoured cars. The German occupiers had disappeared from the region for good.

The Argylls were relieved in Dinteloord by "B" Coy of the Lincoln and Welland Regiment. Contact was made with the 49th British Division, and the Canadians stayed in Dinteloord until 7 November, when they received orders to head for Waalwijk [7].

The Canadians mop up the last resistance

On 5 November, the carrier platoon of the Lincoln and Welland Regiment was sent out on patrol towards the Boompjesdijk (M7). "B" Coy boarded trucks bound for Dinteloord, where they would replace the Argyll and Sutherland Highlanders of Canada. At the bridge across the Dintel, they made contact with the British 49th Division. From that position, patrols of the New Brunswick Rangers were sent off towards Stampersgat, a village southeast of Dinteloord. The carriers reported back at 1420 hrs from their patrol along the Boompjesdijk. They took three prisoners and reported no further incidents.

The 15th Field Regiment RCA, positioned at the southern edge of Steenbergen, moved to Dinteloord during the afternoon to assist the British in the north. A group of approximately one hundred men were sent to a church service in Bergen op Zoom. The rain had once again turned the position south of Dinteloord into a quagmire, and harassing fire was delivered during the night from the direction of Willemstad.

The artillerymen returned to Steenbergen on 7 November and were billeted in civilian housing. The YMCA Auxiliary Services Officer[18] organized a movie show to entertain the soldiers [12].

The engineers reported that all roads were passable and free of mines, but Sapper H.C. Pettit (8 Field Squadron RCE) was critically injured in the course of a recovery operation involving a tank wreck on the Doornedijkje. The tank, belonging to the Foot Guards, had been hit on 30 October. Sapper Pettit died of his wounds on 9 November in the 30th Field Dressing Station in Brasschaet [16].

The 8th Light-Anti Aircraft Regiment RCA near Lepelstraat was taken out of the line and left for Steenbergen / Dinteloord along with the rest of the 4th Armoured Brigade.

The 7th Medium Regiment RCA arrived in Steenbergen around noon on 5 November from their location north of Bergen op Zoom. They positioned their heavy artillery on the right side of Dinteloordse Weg just before the bridge across the Vliet (P9), with one battery putting its guns behind and parallel with the dike. A small landing strip had been constructed from steel planking near the intersection of Stierenweg and Zoekweg in Westland (J14) and there were reports of small planes using this location in the days following 4 November. These were likely AOPs (Air Observation Posts) providing support to the 7th Medium Regiment RCA.

Few spectacular events occurred during two days of shelling, except for the kitchen truck of the 12th Battery, which was destroyed when it hit a mine. The truck delivering hot food also ran into problems when it bogged down in thick mud and almost capsized. History does not record whether the food was still hot when it finally arrived. The 15th Field Regiment left Steenbergen for Bergen op Zoom on the morning of November 7th to shell the Germans elsewhere [35].

The Division rests after the battle

From 5 to 8 November, the battalions of the 10th Brigade (the Algonquin Regiment, the Lincoln and Welland Regiment, and the Argyll & Sutherland Highlanders of Canada) rested in the Steenbergen region.

On 6 November, a fatal accident took place at the home of the De Jong family on Oudlandsestraat. On their return, the De Jongs had found their house filled with Canadians of the Lincoln and Welland Regiment. The men were very well-behaved, and most of them slept in a small abandoned house at the back. During the day, they relaxed or carried out maintenance on the large tank parked beside the De Jong residence. A few men shared the house with the De Jongs. During the day, the officer slept in Grandpa's box bed and at night, Grandpa took his place. The older De Jong daughters basked in the attention from the young soldiers. Daughter Marie had formed a friendship with one of them, Private Milton E. Livingstone. On 6 November, the two were sitting side by side at the table, looking up words in a dictionary in an effort to

---

[18] Every battalion or regiment of the Canadian army had an Auxiliary Services Officer responsible for entertaining the troops. Members of a number of charitable organizations, they were stationed right behind the front lines to organize leisure activities for the men and provide them with refreshments.

learn a little of each other's language. A soldier of American origins (in the interview, Lies de Jong called him "the Texas man") sat across from Marie and Milton, cleaning his weapon. Without warning, the weapon went off, and Milton Livingstone collapsed with a muffled groan. He was fatally injured. Marie watched in horror as her friend's body was wrapped in a grey blanket, taken outside through the window, and removed by a truck. The chaplain of the regiment tried to counsel the family, but the language barrier defied his efforts. Marie kept the picture Milton Livingstone had given her until the day she died, in 2008.

 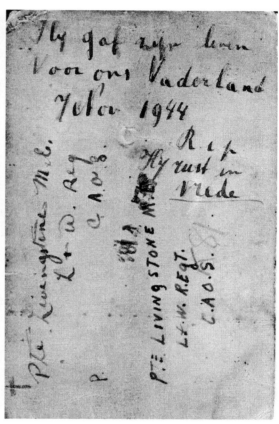

The photo of Private Livingstone that Marie de Jong kept until de day she died.

Reverse of the photo of Private Livingstone (photo A. van Elsakker). The Dutch text reads:
"He gave his life for our fatherland.
7 November 1944. Rest in peace."

After a short period of rest, the 4th Armoured Division liberators moved eastward on 9 November. The front, stretching from Schouwen-Duiveland to the German border, remained stationary throughout the winter, guarded by patrols and thinly-spread observation posts. Steenbergen found itself in a so-called military zone. A curfew was in effect and no free traffic was permitted within 1,500 metres of the Eendracht canal. The coastal region was off-limits except for holders of a special pass, which could be obtained from the O.D. commander.

Christmas card from 1944. The badge on the beret of the Canadian soldier is that of the Manitoba Dragoons (collection P. Adriaansen).

Three observation posts were located near Dinteloord: Post Alpha at the Dintel locks, Charlie near the Carolina polder, and Delta at De Punt. Each post was manned by three soldiers, with order to withdraw to a secondary line as soon as they spotted any Germans. In that event, assault troops would be rushed up from Breda for a counter-attack.

Sporadic shots were exchanged, usually indirect artillery fire, and most of the residents in the area were evacuated in view of the danger. The two opponents sent out the occasional patrol "to the other side" to gather information. All in all, it was a very unpleasant period for the troops. Standing guard duty in the foul weather while nothing happened most of the time, they still had to be prepared for unexpected enemy activity and cope with the stress this imposed [20].

The troops of the 12th Manitoba Dragoons (18th Canadian Armoured Car Regiment) were often seen in Steenbergen during the winter months (November to February). It should be noted that "A" Squadron of this regiment had been added to the 4th Canadian Armoured Division during the fighting in Steenbergen. Unfortunately, no detailed battle information was available at the time of writing. The only reference to the deployment of this squadron is found in the war diary of the 10th Infantry Brigade and in the message log of the 4th Brigade. Historical records suggest that the squadron was deployed on the extreme western flank of the Division, between Halsteren and the Eendracht canal. The first Canadians on the island of Tholen were members of the Dragoons, and the regimental history reports that Corporal J.F. Stanley was killed

Tunic of Private Dyer of the 12th Manitoba Dragoons (collection of the author).

when his vehicle hit a mine. The location and exact time of this incident are unknown, but the date of 1 November suggests that this incident occurred in the vicinity of Steenbergen. Another member of this regiment, Sergeant Turner, lies buried in Bergen op Zoom. The date of death of 30 October suggests that he, too, died north of Bergen op Zoom.

This reconnaissance regiment in their big, armoured vehicles patrolled the front sector from Tholen to Moerdijk during the winter months. Their headquarters were in Roosendaal. Shelling occurred at irregular intervals during this period, wounding several soldiers in Sint-Philipsland. In January, Trooper Veness of the 12th Dragoons was taken by surprise by a German patrol near Fort Sabina. He died on the spot [3].

Tanks parked on the snow-covered market of Steenbergen in the first winter following the liberation. This photo was published in the memorial pamphlet of a Norwegian fighter squadron stationed in Woensdrecht (collection G. van Pul).

The Steenbergen Guard Detachment of the NBS.

Apart from British and Canadian troops, local Dutch guard troops were also active during this period, including the Dutch Third Assault Troop Battalion, which was stationed in the polders near Dinteloord during the winter of 1944/45. A Steenbergen guard detachment of the NBS (Netherlands Interior Forces), commanded by Mr Bastiaansen, patrolled a sector north and south of the Benedensas lock near the hamlet of De Heen. Apart from doing patrol duty, the NBS also guarded the Dutch collaborators who had been locked up in the barracks on the Gummarusvelden road (F5, Map IV). A total of 34 Steenbergen collaborators (members of the National Socialist Movement in the Netherlands) and fifteen other collaborationist Dutch citizens were taken in custody. They were sent to Bergen op Zoom in short order to stand trial.

In the vernacular, these guard troops were called the "O.D." (Orde Dienst, the name of the well-known Dutch war-time resistance movement). In spite of that name, however, few of the original O.D. resistance people served with the guard detachment. Most of the guards were "local boys" from Steenbergen and Welberg. Joining was a simple matter. Once a man reported, he was handed a rifle and put on "active duty" with immediate effect. Uniforms and other military equipment were not available.

Guard post "Francis" on the sea dike near De Heen, winter of 1944. The following members of the local guard detachment of the NBS have been identified: from l. to r. Ko Laros, Gerard Jonkers, Adam de Nijs. In front is Buys, and on the extreme right, wearing wooden shoes and armed with a German rifle, is Marinus Sulkers (photo A. De Nijs).

Nearly all of the patrols took place at night. The young men would march in single file to their designated sector in hopes of discovering signs of German infiltration. Guard posts were constructed along the sea dike from Nieuw Vossemeer to the Dintel locks, and in cooperation with the Allied forces stationed in the region, the posts were manned around the clock. Guard posts were also positioned in areas considered strategically important, such as the Blauwe Sluis (hamlet east of Welberg) and the bridge across the Vliet. In fact, it is fortunate that they never made contact with the enemy, since a group of experienced German soldiers could have inflicted heavy losses on the O.D.

Although the O.D. never encountered any Germans, German patrols certainly did visit the region. A noteworthy incident took place on the Schenkeldijk at the Koetsenruyters' farm. One night, a German patrol stealthily approached the farm and took the family by surprise. The Germans forcibly removed Leen Koetsenruyter, the farmer's son, hoping to obtain military information. Leen was badly beaten during the interrogations but ultimately survived his ordeal.

Welberg resident Govardus (Govert) Helmons was one of the members of the guard detachment. He had returned to Steenbergen by bicycle from his hiding place in Eindhoven about a week after the liberation. The situation in Welberg was appalling. There was no work and nearly everything was wrecked. Joining the O.D. was a relatively easy way to be of some use

Govert Helmons in Indonesia. He served with the Dutch 6th Infantry Regiment, 2nd Batallion (photo: G. Helmons).

Identity card of Govert Helmons of the Steenbergen guard detachment (author's collection).

and earn a bit of money in the process. Govert remembers a patrol to a deserted house on Oostdam right after he "joined up." There was reason to believe that a German soldier was hiding in the house. Together with Piet Geers and Commander Bastiaansen, he entered the house, armed with a flashlight and a rifle. Fortunately, it turned out to be a false alarm.

Several months later, on 1 January 1945, the detachment was on guard duty at Blauwe Sluis. It was the day of the German Luftwaffe's final, massive air raid on the British lines. The

German aircraft were flying at very low altitudes to avoid detection. They were spotted by the men of the O.D. on the way over, and when they returned after the raid, the men were ready for them. Govert Helmons fired a single shot with his Lee-Enfield No. 4, aiming at one of the German aircraft. It proved to be one shot in a million. To his utter amazement, the machine crashed in the polder in the area of Stampersgat. The pilot had been grazed by the bullet and lost control of the aircraft. He survived the crash and was taken to Roosendaal for medical treatment. The commander of the Steenbergen detachment treated Govert Helmons to 200 cigarettes for his amazing achievement, and he received another 200 cigarettes from the district commander in Bergen op Zoom. He was also allowed to paint a white band on his rifle to mark his "kill." After his service with the O.D., he joined the Dutch 6th Infantry Regiment and served in Indonesia.

The Canadians return

On 29 December 1944, the Canadian Grenadier Guards returned to the area with a company of the Lake Superior Regiment. Headquarters were set up in Halsteren. Led by Lieutenant Colonel Pope (commander of the 62nd Anti-Tank Regiment RA, British I Corps), the squadrons were spread across the region, with No. 2 Squadron assigned to a position near Steenbergen. The force was quite extensive, composed of "B" Coy LSR, 36th Battery, 23rd Field Regiment (SP) RCA, and a battery from a British medium regiment. The 36th Battery of the 23rd Field Regiment (SP) RCA, equipped with howitzers mounted on tracked vehicles, fired shots from both the hamlet of Zwarte Ruiter and a position on Noordlangeweg near Dinteloord (QR5). As frost had turned the roads into sheets of ice, the cumbersome vehicles regularly slid off the road and their crews would patiently wait for the recovery vehicle. Shelling was sporadic, and the men spent most of their time near their vehicles on Steenbergen's market square, carrying out maintenance under the fascinated eyes of Steenbergen's youths.

The troops conducted aggressive patrols in Schouwen, and contact was made with the Schouwen resistance. The combined force was relieved by elements of the Polish 1st Armoured Division, which remained in the area during that whole period [20].

V-1s over Steenbergen

In the winter of 1944/45, Steenbergen found itself on the approach route of the German V-1 and V-2 rocket weapons intended to disrupt the port of Antwerp. The Allies organized an anti-aircraft defence shield around Antwerp extending as far as Steenbergen. Anti-aircraft posts manned by American soldiers were positioned on Bergse Grintweg and Hoogstraat, and British searchlight batteries were placed between the American guns. Other guns were located along the Afgeslechtedijk and the Welbergsedijk (Farmer Bogers).

From time to time, a V-1 would land in the vicinity of Steenbergen. One projectile crashed down on 5 March 1945 near Olmendreef. Two others fell near Blauwe Sluis and on Langeweg in the Westland. Another V1 crashed near Blauwe Sluis and failed to explode. The projectile was destroyed shortly afterwards and no further incidents are recorded. The projectiles in the Westland and near Blauwe Sluis crashed in the polder without further incidents. The explosion of the V-1 that fell on Olmendreef, however, took the life of greengrocer Jan van Meer. His brother Koos van Meer lost an arm in the incident. One of the De Bruin children was hit by glass fragments and lost an eye, and seven other people were injured. A police report of the incident states that at 0700, the V-1 was hit by anti-aircraft guns positioned near Steenbergen.

When the projectile was hit, it spun on its axis and crashed to the ground. The explosion occurred in a field 150 metres from Bergse Grintweg and 100 metres from Olmendreef [52].

The end of February 1945 saw the start of the major offensive of the British 21st Army Group at Nijmegen pushing east, and the "Steenbergen front" lost all relevance to the continuation of the campaign. The post-war period of construction and normalization was about to begin.

The civilian situation after the liberation

The liberation of Steenbergen left a trail of destruction in its wake. The area known today as Steenbergen South, right through to Welberg, had been heavily hit. The damage in the rest of Steenbergen was not as severe, although the ravaged Gummarus church bore eloquent witness to the devastation.

One of the three field artillery regiments kept track of its ammunition consumption during the fighting around Steenbergen. The information is given below, to illustrate the intensity of the shelling:

19th Army Field Regiment (SP) RCA	
DATE	NUMBER OF SHELLS FIRED
30/10/1944	949
31/10/1944	1024
01/11/1944	2707
02/11/1944	1243
03/11/1944	3588
04/11/1944	1925
05/11/1944	0

In addition to the 19th Field Regiment (SP) RCA (which officially belonged to the 2nd AGRA), the division had two more similar field artillery regiments (the 15th and the 23rd). Assuming all three regiments fired approximately the same number of shells, calculations based on the above figures indicate that Welberg and Steenbergen South would have been hit on average by between three and six shells per minute.

Housing problems

The township reported 230 properties completely destroyed, 440 buildings heavily damaged, and minor damage to 575 dwellings. There was hardly a house in the Steenbergen-South/Welberg region that still had glass in its window frames or tiles on its roof. The devastation left some

View of the start of Kaaistraat, shortly after the liberation (collection P. Adriaansen).

1,200 people in need of shelter. In some cases, up to three families were forced to share one of the small cottages lining the dikes, and this raised public health concerns. It should be noted that in the fall of 1944, the region had also offered shelter to some 1,200 refugees from the Zeeland and South Holland islands, who had been evacuated following the flooding by the Germans. An

The interior of the ruined Gummarus church (collection P. Adriaansen).

urgent search for alternatives yielded several possibilities, including the canteen of the sugar factory. The German barracks in Slingerbos near Eekelenberg and in Bocht also came in handy. Other people lived in small bunkers in the area called "Villa park" and in barracks near the Gummarusvelden road.

Many residents of Steenbergen made room for homeless families and the presbytery on Kaaistraat was also said to be packed with refugees. Accommodation in De Heen, Kruisland, and Nieuw Vossemeer was also utilized. Since there was little or no alternative, the residents of Welberg and Steenbergen set about rebuilding and repairing their damaged homes. Proper building materials were not available, so people made do

with whatever they could find, using straw and pieces of wreckage to patch the holes. The case of the Cornelius church is a good example. As most of the church was leaking, a wall was built from 280 bales of straw to enclose the altar. This allowed people to attend church during the first few months after the liberation. It was not long, however, before the lice residing in the straw made their presence felt, attacking the churchgoers with such vigour that they grimly endured Mass. The shell holes in the pews are still visible today, as are the wooden patches on the inside of the roof, covering the innumerable shell holes.

Koolbaantje shortly after the liberation. The house with the makeshift wall of straw was occupied by the Van de Branden family. Note the hole in the straw, which served as a window (photo A. Helmons).

Walking through Welberg today, one can still see signs of the repairs made to the older homes to patch shell and bullet holes. Welberg's presbytery and the outer wall of the church also still show signs of numerous repairs. Examples of emergency housing still survive in various locations (Witte Ruiter, Welbergsedijk), bearing witness to the difficult years of reconstruction.

The food situation

Given the agricultural nature of the region, the food situation was not catastrophic at the outset. With all the cattle that had been wounded and killed in battle, meat was initially plentiful. Once that supply dried up, however, it became scarce. Soap was a rare commodity. A soup

kitchen was opened in Steenbergen to distribute the limited food supplies, and residents of Welberg could purchase a meal for 30 cents from Christ van Broekhoven at 4 Corneliusstraat. Various food items remained rationed until 1949.

Picture postcard of Hoogstraat in Welberg shortly after the war (author's collection).

Public health

The medical situation in the township gave the authorities serious cause for concern. The hospital's 50 beds were insufficient to accommodate the large number of patients who had been wounded in the battles, but despite the difficult circumstances, the meagre staff did its best to provide treatment. While supplies were extremely limited during the fighting, the arrival of the liberators brought rapid improvement.

The end of the hostilities did not mean that there were no further casualties. Mines, in particular, took their toll and a number of victims were admitted to hospital. Another outcome of the liberation was an increase in the number of cases of venereal disease.

The poor sanitary conditions caused an outbreak of scabies, and treatment was provided in the White-Yellow Cross centre (a community nursing

Steenbergen children in front of the town hall with aid parcels, probably from the Red Cross Relief Action. The photo was clearly taken shortly after the liberation, since the windows are still boarded up (collection P. Adriaansen).

service facility). The patients were covered in rabies ointment, applied with a large brush, and both they and their clothing were sprayed with an insecticide to combat the lice and flea infestation. It took the health care authorities several months of hard work to raise the medical and hygiene situation to an acceptable level.

Steenbergen residents who fled during the fighting return to town. [16].

The Steenbergen and Welberg Aid Committee

Apart from the official authorities, ordinary people also went into action to help their fellow residents. On 12 November, the "Steenbergen and Welberg Aid Committee" gathered in the town hall for a meeting. Appointed by Mayor van Etten, the 80-member committee had been given the task of distributing clothing, furniture and other items to those who had lost everything in the fighting. In the course of the meeting, chairman Baartmans announced that thanks to the committee's efforts, 250 families in Steenbergen and Welberg had received assistance [21].

The badly damaged Cornelius church in Welberg, 1944 or 1945 (collection C. Slokkers).

Casualties among the civilian population of the township of Steenbergen

As the reader will have noted, known stories of civilian casualties from Welberg have been woven into the story told by this book. The following section lists a number of Welberg residents who were killed in the fighting but whose stories are not known. The names of those who died after the liberation as a direct or indirect result of the war are also included. The information has been reproduced from a memorial leaflet issued on the occasion of the victims' commemoration in 1955. This list is followed by a list of casualties from Steenbergen and Kruisland. For those who fell in Dinteloord, the reader is referred to the 1995 publication by G. van Saarloos entitled "Dinteloord, oorlogsherinneringen" (Dinteloord, War Memories).

From l. to r.: Koos, Ad, and Piet Helmons. The brothers Koos and Piet met a tragic end in 1944 (see below). Photo A Helmons.

Casualties among the population of Welberg

Petrus Raats died on 6 November 1944, aged 61. It is not known how and where he was killed.

Anton Vos died on 13 November 1944. No further details are known.

Jo Gelten in uniform in Indonesia (photo Mrs Iriks).

On 13 November 1944, nine days after the end of the hostilities, the war claimed two more victims. The event is imprinted on Ad Helmons' memory. He was poking around Steenbergen with his two brothers, Piet (12) and Koos (16), as they had been doing for some days. With war supplies scattered all over Steenbergen and no school to attend, they had ample opportunity to examine the wide assortment of interesting "toys." Given their age, the brothers had no idea of the danger they faced. Fate struck as they walked down Oudlandsestraat, close to the tank wall. The two brothers stepped on a mine and died instantly.

Fate also struck the Van den Maagdenberg family. They had been hiding in a shelter near their home on Wipstraat, not far from the intersection with Molenweg. Cornelius, 42, Adriana van den Maagdenberg-Musters, 39, son Henricus (12) and daughter Cornelia (7) were found dead in their shelter a few days after the liberation. The cause of this tragic incident has two versions. The memorial leaflet of 1955 refers to a shell hit, but oral reports mention the collapse of their shelter under the weight of a German SPG.

Adri Gelten, aged 55, was killed on 7 October 1940 by a German bomb dropped on the sugar factory of Stampersgat.

Gerrend de Jong, aged 20, lived on the Welbergsedijk road. He was transported to a forced labour camp in Stuttgart, Germany and died of disease on 13 July 1945 in the St. Franciscus Hospital in Strasbourg. He is buried in the Dutch War Cemetery in Orry-la-Ville, 29 km north-east of Paris (grave A-3-11).

Johannus Gelten (Jo van Dijk, according to the birth register), aged 21, served with the Dutch 3rd Infantry Regiment in Indonesia, where he was killed on 21 December 1949 near Cimaung. He died accidentally while on patrol, firing a mortar. The shell exploded as it left the barrel and fragments hit him in the head and chest. He died instantly.

Cornelius van der Weegen, aged 19, died on 15 November 1946 near Batavia (Jakarta) while serving in the Dutch army in Indonesia. A dispatch rider, he is reported to have died when his motorcycle hit a wire strung across the road.

Petrus Jonkers, aged 23, died in the German penal camp of Ommen on 14 February 1943. He had been arrested by the authorities for theft and sentenced to one year of forced labour.

The grave of Cornelius (Kees) van der Weegen in Indonesia in 1949 (collection P. Adriaansen).

Jacobus van de Klundert, aged 16, shared the same fate. He, too, had been arrested for theft and sentenced to one year of forced labour. He died in Zwolle, during an Allied bombing raid.

Adrianus de Groen-Rommens became ill in 1940 while in military service. He died on 11 January 1945 in the Central Hospital in Amsterdam after a long illness. He was 26 years old.

Petrus (Peter) Gabriëls-van Terheijden died in hospital at the age of 60 on 19 November 1944. According to the local newspaper of 24 November 1944, he died as a result of serious internal injuries suffered in a fall off the roof of his farm house on the Welbergsedijk. The 1955 memorial publication refers to a fatal injury caused by a shell fragment. Peter Gabriëls was probably hit in the back by a shell fragment and died of the combined effects of his wound and the fall from the roof.

Grave of Gerrend de Jong in Orry-la-Ville, France (photo Oorlogs-gravenstichting)

Civilian victims in Steenbergen and Kruisland

The first edition of the "Steenbergse Courant" (a local newspaper) published after the liberation contained a list of the Steenbergen victims [50]. Their names and the circumstances of their deaths, as far as they are known, are given below:

- ❖ Leonardus Heijnen, aged 22 (De Heen), was killed on 31 October 1944. He died in his sleep when a shell fragment penetrated his bedroom in his parents' home.

- ❖ Alphonsius van der Riet, aged 52 (Steenbergen), and his housekeeper Mathilda Boenne, aged 64 (Halsteren) both died on 4 November 1944. The two, travelling in a horse-drawn cart, hit a mine between Westlandse Langeweg and Witte Ruijter.

- ❖ Petronilla van der Pas, aged 47 (Steenbergen), died on 2 November 1944.

- ❖ Sacharias van den Berg, aged 64 (Kruisland), died on 31 October 1944 in Halsteren while a British soldier was clearing mines. Twenty-three mines exploded in this incident, which also killed the British soldier. The cause of the explosion is unknown.

- ❖ Marinus Buckens, aged 37 (Kruisland), died on 30 October 1944. Killed instantly by a land mine on the Leemput road (Sacharias van den Berg was Marinus' father-in-law).

- ❖ Adriana van den Berg-de Backer, aged 27 (Kruisland), died on 31 October 1944 in the same incident in which Sacharias van den Berg lost his life.

- ❖ Petrus Adriaansen, aged 36 (Kruisland), died on 29 October 1944. He was hit by a shell fragment in his home on Roosendaalseweg.

- ❖ Maria van de Kasteele, aged 45 (Steenbergen), died on 31 October 1944.

- ❖ Alphonsus van Bavel, aged 43 (Steenbergen), died on 29 October 1944. He was beheaded by a shell fragment on his farm on Boswijkdreef.

- ❖ Adrianus van Bergen, aged 33 (Wouw), died on 7 November 1944.

- ❖ Adrianus van Oevelen, aged 50 (Steenbergen), died on 31 October 1944.

- ❖ Johannes Dekkers, aged 32 (Steenbergen), died on 29 October 1944.

- ❖ Johannus van Dongen, aged 41 (Steenbergen), died on 1 November 1944.

- ❖ Adrianus Antes, aged 57 (Kruisland), died on 31 October 1944. He suffered critical injuries to his left thigh in his home on Wildenhoek and died in hospital in Oud- and Nieuw-Gastel.

- ❖ Cornelius A.A. Aanraad, aged 20 (Kruisland), died in October 1944 of extreme physical abuse suffered in a forced-labour camp in Germany.

This section presents a brief analysis of the hostilities around Steenbergen and Welberg.

Roughly speaking, the operation near Steenbergen can be divided into the following episodes:

- o *30 October.* The Germans retreat to the Steenbergen "stronghold." Their objective is to hold up the Allied advance long enough to evacuate all materiel and men via Dintelsas, Willemstad, and Zijpe.

- o *31 October.* The advance of the 4th Armoured Brigade stops at the Witte Ruiter bridge. The advance via Oudlandsestraat loses momentum.

- o *1 November.* The Oudlandsestraat route is selected to break through the defensive line. The Algonquins attempt a night attack and are forced back. The 10th Infantry Brigade takes over the attack.

- o *2 November.* The 10th Infantry Brigade attacks in the same sector with a classic plan: two battalions in front, one in reserve, and the customary artillery preparation.

- o *3 November.* The Germans elect to withdraw since the line on the Mark river east of Steenbergen has been breached. The Canadians cautiously advance across the full width of their front sector.

Why did it take so long to liberate Steenbergen?

The central question is why the 4th Canadian Armoured Division had so much difficulty dislodging the Germans from their defensive line around Steenbergen. Based on a quantitative and qualitative comparison, one would have expected the Canadians to be able to roll up the German defence in no more than a few hours. Yet the 4th Canadian Armoured Division was held up for *five days*, permitting the Germans to evacuate precious supplies and war materiel across the Hollands Diep. From a military tactical perspective, therefore, the German plan to delay the Canadian advance can be seen as having succeeded. From a strategic point of view, however, the Germans were in a hopeless situation. They did not have a hope of stemming the tide of war, and from a rational perspective, resistance was completely pointless.

At first glance, the quantitative superiority of the Canadians does indeed seem overwhelming. A more detailed analysis shows, however, that the Canadian superiority should be put into perspective: at the end of October/early November, the Algonquins were short 250 men [44]. Officially, each company had around 100 men who could actually "eyeball" the enemy. Assuming that all replacements they requested were for soldiers at the front, the average strength per company was around 40 men. Extrapolated to the 10th Infantry Brigade (three infantry battalions with four companies), the actual fighting strength of the infantry was probably around 500 men. The armoured regiments of the 4th Armoured Brigade, on the other hand, were at full strength, as regards both men and vehicles. (The Lake Superior Regiment probably had the same problem as the other infantry battalions).

In terms of manpower, the German strength was approximately equal, but the big difference was that the Germans had neither reserves nor support troops. It should also be noted that the Germans, with their limited manpower, had to guard a broader front than the Canadians. Their area of concentration ran from Glymes to Blauwe Sluis, whereas the Canadians concentrated in the Oudland area. The German (tank) armaments and ammunition supplies amounted to a fraction of those on the Canadian side. The Germans fought with their backs against the wall, so to speak.

Taking into account the Canadian infantry problems referred to above, the actual superiority of the Canadians was probably a factor of three to two.

In the opinion of the author, the answer to the question of why the Canadians had so much difficulty with the German defensive line relates to the following aspects:

o The Canadians lacked a clear attack objective and thus did not have a clear plan. This generated hesitation.

o The Canadians underestimated the Germans' tactical knowledge and skills. As a result, the attack lacked proper preparation. Knowledge of the enemy's strength and/or weakness was not put to good use.

o The Canadians failed to make the most of their superiority in materiel (especially tanks). Time after time, the division's strength was dissipated across a broad front and units were sent off to fight the enemy on their own.

o The marshy, open polder landscape where the fighting took place was greatly to the advantage of the static defenders.

o The Germans had a very narrow objective ("delay the enemy's advance"), a goal that is reputedly achievable with limited means.

o The Germans consistently concentrated their very limited means in the right place at the right time.

In summary, the Germans prepared an excellent defensive position, making maximum use of the terrain. They employed veteran soldiers and were able to concentrate their forces at key times during the battle. The Canadians, for their part, held numerical superiority, but not to the ideal ratio required for an attack on a prepared position. Their ranks also numbered many raw recruits who lacked combat experience. In addition, the terrain favoured the defensive forces due to the canalizing nature of the approach to Steenbergen and the polder countryside. It is in the combination of these factors that one should seek the answer to the question of why it took the Canadians four days to liberate Welberg and Steenbergen.

The importance of the Battle of Steenbergen in a broader perspective

In light of the overall liberation campaign, the importance of the fighting described in this publication was relatively minor. The Germans were already beaten and most of the supplies of the German 15th Army were already north of the Hollands Diep. At the time the Canadians were in Welberg, Germany did not have a hope of stemming the tide of war. Whereas any right-minded person would have long given up on the lost battle, the German military apparatus under

Hitler carried on fighting. The only result was that the casualty lists of both friend and foe grew steadily longer.

The loss of lives on the Canadian side in relation to the strategic importance of the operation was very high, the more so since there were not enough men available to replace the casualties. Every Canadian soldier who saw combat in Europe was a volunteer, and by the end of the summer of 1944, the numbers of new recruits were insufficient to replace war casualties, particularly among the infantry. In many instances, drivers, gunners, and various other non-infantry soldiers were rushed to the front after an abbreviated and woefully inadequate refresher course. Many of these ill-prepared and inexperienced soldiers did not last long in battle. Indeed, of all the Algonquin soldiers who were wounded or killed in Welberg, 80% had joined the regiment only at the end of September. These raw recruits had virtually no combat experience and in some cases, they were killed even before their names could be recorded by their unit.

In conclusion

The official history of the Canadian army devotes no more than a few lines to Welberg. The Algonquins describe their part in the battle in great detail in "Warpath," their regimental history. Other postwar publications also contain fragments of the battle, but to the author's knowledge, no detailed study presenting a complete and detailed account of *all* the events has ever been published in the 65 years since the end of the war. As stated in the introduction, the author hopes that the account presented in this book will bring back memories for the veterans and enlighten the families and especially the grandchildren of those who fought in this area. In Welberg, as in the rest of the Netherlands, the Canadians, our liberators, gained an almost god-like status, and regardless of how one views the reasons, benefits, and exact circumstances of the events that took place, the fact remains that dozens of Canadians who fell here will forever rest in Dutch soil. It is up to the post-war generation to cherish their memory.

They shall not grow old, as we that are left grow old:

Age shall not weary them, nor the years condemn.

At the going down of the sun and in the morning

We will remember them. We will remember them

Laurence Binyon, 1914.

Appendices

I.   Names, terms, and abbreviations

II.   The 4th Canadian Armoured Division

III.   War monuments in and near Steenbergen

IV.   Canadian casualties in the battle of Welberg and Steenbergen

V.   German casualties in the battle of Steenbergen

VI.   Decorations awarded to Canadian soldiers in the Battle of Steenbergen

VII.   Sources consulted

VIII.   List of maps

IX.   Index of names of persons

Appendix I: Abbreviations, terms, and proper names

This work contains numerous geographical references, military terms, and abbreviations that may impede comprehension. To orient and assist the reader, the lists below provide map references where possible and brief descriptions of terms and abbreviations.

Names of towns and villages, streets, and geographical features

(Unless otherwise specified, the coordinates refer to Map III on p. 9).

Name	Description	Map reference
Afgeslechtedijk	Dike/road east of Steenbergen (Map IV)	M3
Bergse Grintweg	Street in Steenbergen. Now Fransenweg / Burgemeester van Loonstraat (Map IV)	D7–11
Bergsewater	See Ligne	
Blauwe Sluis	Hamlet east of Welberg	Q10
Bocht	Hamlet just south of Welberg, where the Boomvaart crosses the road (Map IV)	J10
Boomdijk	Dike/road south of Welberg (Map IV)	P14-R17
Boomvaart	Peat canal (dug in 1643)	N12-P15
Boswijkdreef	Road south of Welberg	P16
Breede Watergang	Canal	H9
Corneliusstraat	Street in Welberg (Map IV)	K8
Handwijzer, De	Café at the intersection of the road to Lepelstraat and Steenbergseweg	J16
De Heen	Hamlet northeast of Steenbergen	H8
De Overval	Hamlet NE of Welberg near De Weel	P10
De Weel	Pond between Steenbergen and Blauwe Sluis	Q10
Dwarsdijk	Dike connecting the Boomdijk and the Groenedijk, today known as Canadezenweg (Canadians Road) (Map IV)	N10
Eekelenberg	Name of a farm owned by the Loos family (Map IV)	G11
Eekelendreef	Road off Moerstraatseweg	M13
Eendracht	(Schelde-Rijnkanaal) Former name of the waterway between Tholen and Brabant	C12-E16
Groenedijk	Dike/road south of Welberg (Map IV)	N8
Halsters Laag	Wetlands area	M16-L14/15
Halsterseweg	Road between Steenbergen and Halsteren	J16-L13
Hoogstraat	Road from Welberg to the southern tip of Steenbergen (Map IV)	J9-F10
Kinderbaantje	Street in Welberg (Map IV)	J9
Kladde	Hamlet southwest of Steenbergen	H14
Kleine Kerkstraat	Street in Steenbergen (Map IV)	F5
Klutsdorp	Village SSW of Steenbergen	K16
Koolbaantje	Former street in the southern tip of Steenbergen, now Brooijmansdreef (Map IV)	D10-11
Krabben	Region.	N14

Kromwielswegje	Road south of Welberg	P13
Laurentiusdijk	Dike/road bordering Welberg on the east (Map IV)	K7
Lepelstraat	Village	H15-16
Ligne	River	L15-K12
Mariadijk	Dike/road north of Steenbergen	N9
Moerstraatseweg	Former Oudlandsestraat	N16 -M14
Moerstraten	Town just off the map, at the end of Moerstraatseweg.	P18
Molenweg	Road in Steenbergen (Map IV)	F6-H6
Oudemolen	Village just off the map, at the northern tip of Halsteren.	J16
Oudlandsdijkje	Dike/road south of Steenbergen	L14-N16
Oudlandsestraat	Now Moerstraatseweg	N16 -M14
Oudlandse Watergang	Drainage canal from the Halsters Wetlands to the Boomvaart and via a culvert to De Weel. It crosses Moerstraatseweg	M14
Polderwatergang	Polder drainage canal	P13
Ruiter, Witte	Name of a bridge across the Ligne river	K14
Ruiter, Zwarte	Hamlet east of Steenbergen	J11
Vliet	River north of Steenbergen	F5 – N8
Waterhoefke	Hamlet south of Steenbergen, east of the Ligne	M14
Welbergsedijk	Dike/road east of Steenbergen	M7
Westland	Region	JK / 12 13
Westlandse Langeweg	Road west of Steenbergen (Map IV)	A9-E9
Wipstraat	Street in Welberg, today Kapelaan Kockstraat (Map IV)	G8-H9
Zoom	River near Bergen op Zoom	

Note: *dijk/dijkje* = dike; *straat* = street; *weg/wegje* = road; *dreef* = avenue; *baantje*= path; *sas* = lock; *watergang* = waterway

Military terminology

Indirect artillery fire: Aiming and firing a gun without relying on a direct line of sight between the gun and its target. The target is triangulated by means of a complex system of map coordinates and predictive calculations of the projectile trajectory.

Barrage: A prolonged concentration of artillery fire directed at a previously determined set of targets.

Harassing fire: Artillery fire directed at predetermined target at irregular intervals. Usually, the targets are main road junctions or built-up areas in which enemy activity is expected.

Bailey bridges: The classification "50' DS" refers to a bridge 50 feet in length constructed of trusses formed by two single panels pinned together side-by-side. This was known as a "Double-Single." Detailed information is available at http://www.fhwa.dot.gov/bridge/prefab/psbsreport03.cfm.

Abbreviations:

AFR	Army Field Regiment
AGRA	Army Group Royal Artillery
AlgR	Algonquin Regiment. Infantry regiment of the 4th Armoured Division.
AOP	Air Observation Post. Small aircraft used for aerial reconnaissance and to direct artillery fire by radioing the enemy positions to the artillery units.
ASHofC	Argyll and Sutherland Highlanders of Canada. Infantry regiment of the 4th Armoured Division.
A/T	Anti-Tank (Regiment). Equipped with anti-tank guns to destroy enemy tanks.
BCR	(28 CAR) British Columbia Regiment. Tank regiment of the 4th Armoured Division.
CAR	Canadian Armoured Regiment
CARR	Canadian Armoured Reconnaissance Regiment
CGG	(22 CAR) Canadian Grenadier Guards. Tank regiment of the 4th Armoured Division.
Coy	Company
Coys	Companies
FLAK	*Flieger Abwehr Kanone.* German term for anti-aircraft gun. The acronym is used in English to denote anti-aircraft fire.
FOO	Forward Observation Officer. Artillery officer attached to the infantry, along with a small group of gunners, and equipped with a radio. The FOO directs the fire of an artillery unit from a forward position. His observations allow the unit to place effective fire.
FR	Field Regiment
FS	Field Squadron
GGFG	(21 CAR) Governor General's Foot Guards. Tank regiment of the 4th Armoured Division.
LAA	Light Anti-Aircraft. Artillery unit armed with anti-aircraft guns to destroy enemy aircraft.

LSR   Lake Superior Regiment. Motorized infantry battalion of the 4th Armoured Division.

L&W   Lincoln and Welland Regiment. Infantry regiment of the 4th Armoured Division.

M10   Tank destroyer. Lightly armoured, tracked vehicle equipped with a 17-pounder gun, tasked to destroy enemy tanks.

NBR   New Brunswick Rangers. Machine gun company of the 4th Armoured Division.

O.D.   "Orde Dienst." Underground organization founded by Dutch ex-military at the beginning of the war to maintain law and order immediately following the fall of Germany.

R   Regiment

RCA   Royal Canadian Artillery

RCE   Royal Canadian Engineers

SAR   (29 CARR) South Alberta Regiment, also referred to as the South Albertas. Reconnaissance regiment of the 4^e Armoured Division

SPG   Self-propelled gun. An armoured, motorized gun mounted on a tracked chassis. Similar to a tank, but more lightly armoured and not necessarily designed as an anti-tank weapon. The SPGs were meant to support the infantry.

Appendix II: The 4th Canadian Armoured Division

To acquaint the reader with the Canadian units that fought in the battle of Steenbergen, this section presents a summary and brief history of the 4th Canadian Armoured Division [4, 5, 9, 17, 19, 23, 24, 25, 32].

From creation to disbandment

The 4th Canadian Armoured Division was created as an infantry division in May 1940. The patch used by the division was a 2 by 3 inch, dark-green rectangle (worn horizontally). The green division patches were worn on both sleeves by all members of the division.

In 1942, the decision was made to convert the infantry division to an armoured division. At that time, an armoured division consisted of two armoured brigades and did not have an infantry component. Overnight, the infantry battalions of the 4th Division became armoured troops. This explains the long names of the regiments, such as the 22nd Canadian Armoured Regiment (Canadian Grenadier Guards). The division shipped out to England in 1942, but it was not until 1943, following a major reorganization of the army, that the division gained its final composition of one armoured brigade and one infantry brigade. The battalions that were to constitute the 10th Infantry Brigade arrived in England in 1943.

The division was transported to France in July 1944 and saw its first action between Caen and Falaise. It played an important part in the encirclement of the German army at Falaise. Following the German defeat at Falaise, the division set off in pursuit of the fleeing Germans and rapidly drove them out of France. The first noteworthy resistance was encountered near Bruges, Belgium, in September. From Bruges, the enemy was driven back towards the east. In September and early October 1944, the division defended the Leopold canal south of Zeeland Flanders. In mid-October, the tanks were deployed from Esschen to Steenbergen in operation "Suitcase." The ensuing lengthy period of patrolling the Maas (sector Waalwijk to Den Bosch) was interrupted by the battle of Kapelseveer at the end of January, in operation "Elephant." In late February 1945, the division took part in the major offensive near Kleef and Udem in Germany, and after crossing the Rhine, it pushed through to the German Plain via the eastern part of the Netherlands (Twente Kanaal, Almelo, and eventually Coevorden). No serious resistance was met after the Kuestenkanal and the division celebrated Germany's capitulation in the vicinity of Oldenburg. With the war at an end, the division was stationed near Almelo in the Netherlands, awaiting repatriation. By the end of December 1945, nearly everyone had returned to Canada, and on 27 December, the division was ordered disbanded.

Strength and weaponry

The organizational strength of a Canadian armoured division was around 15,000 men. Each brigade commanded roughly 3,500 men and the remainder were divided among the support troops. An armoured regiment consisted of approximately 800 men and seventy tanks divided in three squadrons. In the Guards regiments, the squadrons were numbered from 1 to 3, in the other armoured regiments they were known as "A," "B," and "C" squadron. The infantry had battalions (equivalent to an armoured regiment) of around 800 men. A regiment or battalion was commanded by a lieutenant colonel.

The infantry battalions were divided into four companies, "A" through "D," commanded by a Major.

The smallest battle formation in the armoured forces was a troop (led by a lieutenant with four tanks) or a platoon (led by a lieutenant with around 25 men). The artillery regiment's battery was equivalent to a company.

The actual strength at Steenbergen was almost certainly much reduced. Significant losses had been inflicted in the course of the campaign and there was a shortage of replacement troops.

The total number of tanks in a division was around 350, including light reconnaissance tanks. The main battle tank was the American M4 Sherman equipped with a 75 mm gun. The German tanks were far superior to the Shermans in terms of both armour and armament, so in the course of the campaign, one in four Sherman tanks was fitted with a 17-pounder gun to match the Germans. This conversion was known as the Sherman "Firefly."

It should be noted, incidentally, that the tanks sent to the armoured regiments in need of replacements came complete with crews. The crew members were temporarily assigned to "B" Squadron of the Elgin Regiment (St. Thomas, Ontario) for training.

The troops in the Division were all highly motorized. The artillery in 23 Field Regiment (SP) RCA possessed twenty-four mobile 25-pounder howitzers (Sextons). The 15th Field Regiment RCA, attached to the 10th Infantry Brigade, was equipped with regular, towed 25-pounder gun-howitzers. Twenty-four mobile M10 tank destroyers armed with 17-pounder anti-tank guns had been assigned to the anti-tank artillery. The anti-aircraft artillery had a small number of 40 mm mechanized guns. All in all, more than 1,300 trucks and in excess of 250 armoured vehicles were in use.

A division-level summary of Operation "Suitcase" (20 October – 6 November 1944) illustrates the scale of the division, the supply requirements, and the intensity of 17 days' action [38, 5]:

A total of 1,495 Germans were taken prisoner. The number of German casualties was estimated at 2,500. Canadian losses were 164 killed, 648 wounded, and 96 missing in action. [most of them taken prisoner by the Germans]

Six self-propelled assault guns, one tank, eight anti-tank guns, three infantry guns, and one bulldozer were destroyed, as well as seven anti-aircraft guns, five armoured vehicles, twelve trucks, one reconnaissance vehicle, and thirteen cattle trucks.

After seventeen days of fighting, 36 tanks were written off, including anti-tank guns. In all, 3,600 75 mm shells, 1,600 17-pounder shells, and 527 anti-tank shells were fired. The New Brunswick Rangers fired 2,400 4.2 inch mortar shells and 230,000 machine gun bullets. Eight hundred 3 inch mortar shells, 100,383 25-pounder shells, and 6,192 medium calibre artillery shells were expended. The engineers erected 11 bridges, filled 33 craters in roads, destroyed fifteen road obstructions, and checked 180 kilometres of roadside shoulders for mines. They cleared 5,500 kilos of explosives and 500 mines. The signals troops laid around four hundred kilometres of signal wire.

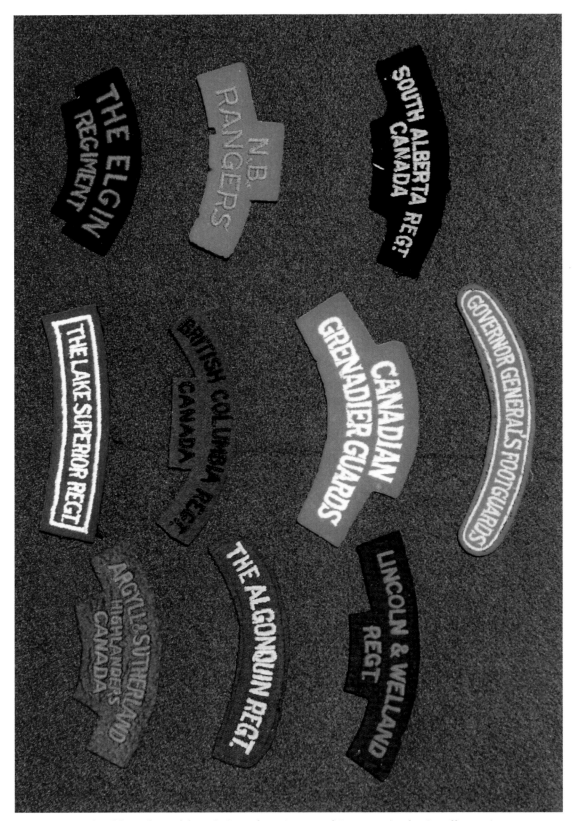

Shoulder titltes of the 4th Canadian Armoured Division (author's collection)

Composition of the division staff

During the episode in Steenbergen, the staff of the 4th Armoured Division consisted of the following officers. Maj. Gen. Harry W. Foster was in overall command. He was assisted by Lieutenant Colonel F.E. Wigle (General Staff Officer grade 1). Logistics management was in the hands of Lieutenant Colonel J.W. Proctor. The division's artillery units were commanded by Brigadier J.N. Lane. Lieutenant Colonel W.P. Shirreff commanded the signals troops, and the engineers were under the command of Lieutenant Colonel J.R.B. Jones.

The following units were under the direct command of the divisional headquarters:

- 4th Armoured Divisional Signals, Royal Canadian Corps of Signals (*all units had their own section of signals troops, assigned to them for the duration of the campaign*)
- 4th Field Security Section, Canadian Intelligence Corps
- 8th Provost Company, Canadian Provost Corps (Military Police)
- 4th Armoured Division Postal Unit, Canadian Postal Corps

The 4th Canadian Armoured Brigade

The 4th Armoured Brigade, under the command of Brigadier R.W. Moncel, consisted of a headquarters with a guard section, three armoured regiments, and one armoured infantry battalion.

21st Canadian Armoured Regiment (Governor General's Foot Guards)

The Foot Guards (formed in 1872) are a militia infantry regiment based in Ottawa, Ontario. They mount the guard on Parliament Hill in Ottawa, dressed in their traditional uniforms of scarlet tunics and large, bearskin caps. The term "Guards" originates in Great Britain, where it is used in reference to a number of regiments that provide guard support for the British Sovereign. Since Canada was a British dominion populated primarily by the British, old British traditions were carried on in the "new" Canada. On 12 June 1940, the regiment recruited an infantry battalion for the active Canadian army. In January 1942, the battalion was converted to an armoured regiment and the name changed to 21 Canadian Armoured Regiment (Governor General's Foot Guards). The regiment was commanded by Lieutenant Colonel E.M. Smith.

22nd Canadian Armoured Regiment (Canadian Grenadier Guards)

The Grenadier Guards, based in Montreal, was formed in 1764 after the British defeated the French. In 1912, the infantry regiment received its official title of Canadian Grenadier Guards. Like the Foot Guards, it performs ceremonial guard duties dressed in traditional uniforms; it takes part in the Changing of the Guard ceremony at Rideau Hall in Ottawa during the summer months.

An active battalion was raised on 3 June 1940, and in January 1942, the infantrymen of the Grenadier guards were also retrained as tank soldiers. The name was changed to 22 Canadian Armoured Regiment (Canadian Grenadier Guards). The commanding officer during the battle of Steenbergen was Lieutenant Colonel W.W. Halpenny.

28th Canadian Armoured Regiment (British Columbia Regiment)

This infantry regiment from Vancouver, British Columbia, was formed in 1920 by amalgamating a number of existing units. It mobilized on 26 August 1939 as the British Columbia Regiment (Duke of Connaught's Own rifles). In January 1942, this regiment, too, acquired tanks and its name was changed to 28 Canadian Armoured Regiment (British Columbia Regiment). The regiment's commanding officer was Lieutenant Colonel C.E. Parish.

Lake Superior Regiment (Motor)

The Lake Superior Regiment is an infantry regiment from Port Arthur (Ontario) on Lake Ontario. The regiment was formed in 1920 from the 52nd battalion Canadian Expeditionary Force, which fought overseas in WWI. A battalion was mobilized for active service on 5 June 1940. In February it was converted to an armoured infantry battalion. Essentially an infantry battalion, it was equipped with armoured vehicles to allow it to follow the tanks in battle. In Steenbergen, this battalion did not fight as a unit. The companies were divided among the armoured regiments. The commanding officer was Lieutenant Colonel R.A. Keane.

Tunic of an unidentified sergeant of the British Columbia Regiment.

10th Canadian Infantry Brigade

The 10th Brigade led by Brigadier J.C. Jefferson commanded three infantry battalions, the division reconnaissance regiment, and a machine gun-mortar company. The headquarters was defended by the 10th Defence and Employment Platoon (Lorne Scots). The Lorne Scots (Brampton, Ontario) supplied defence platoons for all infantry brigade headquarters in all divisions. (Note: During the liberation of Steenbergen, two troops of the Fife and Forfar Yeomanry were attached to the brigade for a period of two days. This unit was equipped with flame-throwing tanks, the so-called "Churchill Crocodiles." The unit formed part of 31 Armoured Brigade, 79 Armoured Division).

Algonquin Regiment

The Algonquin regiment (from northern Ontario) was formed by joining the Algonquin Rifles and the Northern Pioneers in 1936. The regiment mobilized an active battalion on 24 May 1940, and after serving in Newfoundland, it was dispatched to England in June 1943. The battalion was commanded by Lieutenant Colonel R.A. Bradburn.

29th Canadian Armoured Reconnaissance Regiment (South Alberta Regiment)

The South Alberta Regiment was formed in Medicine Hat, Alberta in May 1940 from five western Canada militia units: the 19th Alberta Dragoons, the 15th Alberta Light Horse, the South Alberta Regiment, the Calgary Regiment (tank), and the Edmonton Fusiliers. The regiment mobilized as an infantry regiment, for which each of the founding regiments supplied a company. In February 1942, they were added to the armoured troops and equipped with tanks. Ultimately, they were attached to the 4th Armoured Division as the 29th Canadian Armoured Reconnaissance Regiment (South Alberta Regiment). In terms of armament, a reconnaissance regiment differed little from a conventional armoured regiment. In the battle of Steenbergen, the reconnaissance regiment divided its squadrons among the three infantry battalions. The commanding officer was Lieutenant Colonel G. D. de Salaberry Wotherspoon.

Lincoln and Welland Regiment

During the major military reorganization of 1936, two regiments (the Lincoln Regiment and the Lincoln and Welland Regiment) were joined to form the Lincoln and Welland Regiment. This infantry regiment (St. Catharines, Ontario) mobilized on 1 September 1939. After seeing service in Canada and Newfoundland, the battalion was transported to England in July 1943. The battalion was commanded by Lieutenant Colonel W.T. Cromb.

Argyll and Sutherland Highlanders of Canada

This infantry regiment from Hamilton, Ontario, has a Scottish tradition. Since the regiment was formed in 1903, its members have proudly worn the traditional kilts, glengarries, and balmorals. Naturally, a pipe band is part of the tradition. The regiment mobilized in 1940 and served a year in Jamaica before being dispatched to England in July 1943. The battalion was led by Lieutenant Colonel J.D. Stewart.

10th Independent Machine Gun Company (New Brunswick Rangers)

The New Brunswick Rangers (Sussex, New Brunswick) mobilized on 1 January 1941 and after serving in Labrador, the regiment was transported to England in 1943. To their dismay, the battalion was reduced to less than half of its strength and reorganized as the 10th Machine Gun Company. The weapons they received were the heavy .303 inch Vickers machine guns (three platoons) and the heavy 4.2 inch mortar (one platoon). They were led by Major Bastin during the campaign.

Royal Canadian Artillery

The headquarters of the divisional artillery had a variety of regiments under its command as well as a small group of so-called Counter Mortar Officers and Counter Battery Officers, who gathered information about the location of enemy mortars.

The 15th Field Regiment

The 15th Field Regiment mobilized in 1940. The regiment consisted of three batteries: the 17th (Winnipeg), the 95th (Calgary), and the 110th (Broadview). Its task was to support the 10th Infantry Brigade. They were equipped with 25-pounder gun-howitzers. The regiment was commanded by Lieutenant Colonel R.H.E. Walker.

The 23rd Field Regiment (Self Propelled)

The 23rd Field Regiment, consisting of the 31st (Toronto), the 36th (Cobourg), and the 83rd (Niagara district) batteries, was converted to a self-propelled artillery regiment on 15 May 1943. The regiment was assigned to the 4th Armoured Brigade. They were completely motorized with self-propelled, 25-pounder gun-howitzers (Sextons). The commanding officer was Lieutenant Colonel R.E. Hogarth.

The 8th Light Anti-Aircraft Regiment

In January 1942, the 16th Field Regiment became the 8th Light Anti-Aircraft Regiment with the 70th (Brandon), the 102nd (Dundas) and the 101st (Moosomin) batteries. Armed with 40 mm Bofors anti-aircraft guns, some of them self-propelled, they protected the division against aerial attacks. The regiment was commanded by Lieutenant Colonel McCormack.

Tunic of an unidentified Captain of the 15th Field Regiment.

The 5th Anti-Tank Regiment

The 5th Anti-Tank Regiment mobilized in 1941 with the 96th (Edmonton), 65th (Grenfell), and 3rd (Gananoque) batteries. In January 1943, an additional battery was added to the regiment (the 14th Battery). Since the battery was mobilized in England, the men arrived from all points of the compass and from various units, which explains its nickname "Rainbow" Battery. The 96th and 14th batteries were armed with the M10 "Achilles," a self-propelled, 17-pounder anti-tank gun. The 65th and 3rd batteries were equipped with 17-pounder anti-tank guns towed by White Motor Co. M3A1 armoured vehicles. The commanding officer was Lieutenant Colonel D.S. Harkness (who was appointed Minister of National Defence in October 1960).

In addition to the above units, which officially belonged to the division, a number of extra artillery units were added to the division:

The 19th (Army) Field Regiment

The 19th Field Regiment consisted of the 55th (London), the 63rd (Guelph), and the 99th (Wingham) Batteries. The regiment was mobilized in 1941 and served in Canada until 1943.

During the landing in Normandy, the regiment was part of the first attack wave. Officially, the regiment belonged to the 2nd Canadian AGRA (Army Group Royal Artillery). During the campaign in France, the Netherlands, and Germany, it was usually added to the 4th Armoured Division. The regiment was armed with 25-pounder gun-howitzers.

The 7th Medium Regiment

The 7th Medium Regiment with the 12th (London), the 45th (Lindsay), and the 97th (Walkerton) batteries, mobilized in 1939. The regiment was part of the 2nd Canadian AGRA. During the fighting in Steenbergen, the 2nd Canadian AGRA saw action in Zeeland Flanders. The 7th Medium Regiment was temporarily assigned to 59 AGRA to reinforce the eastern flank of II Canadian Corps. The regiment was armed with 5.5 inch guns.

The 59th AGRA (Army Group Royal Artillery)

The 59th AGRA was an ad-hoc formation consisting of the artillery headquarters of the 59th British Infantry Division and three medium artillery regiments. The 59th Division was dissolved in August 1944 to free up personnel to reinforce other divisions. During Operation "Suitcase," the AGRA comprised two medium British artillery regiments (84 and 112 Medium Regiments RA) and the 7th Medium Regiment RCA mentioned earlier. The AGRA fell under the direct command of the British I Corps.

Royal Canadian Engineers

The military engineering headquarters (4th Armoured Division Headquarters, Divisional Engineering, under the Commander, Royal (Canadian) Engineers (CRE), controlled the following units:

- 6 Field Park Squadron
- 8 Field Squadron
- 9 Field Squadron

Royal Canadian Army Service Corps

Uniform of an unidentified soldier of the Royal Canadian Army Service Corps.

The headquarters of the transport and supply troops (4th Armoured Division Headquarters, Royal Canadian Army Service Corps, under the Commander, Royal (Canadian) Army Service Corps (CRCASC), controlled the following units:

- 4 Armoured Divisional Troops Company
- 4 Armoured Divisional Transport Company
- 4 Armoured Brigade Transport Company
- 10 Infantry Brigade Transport Company

Royal Canadian Army Medical Corps

The medical troops, under the direction of the Assistant Director of Medical Services (ADMS – the senior officer at the division level), was responsible for the treatment and transport of the wounded. They were organized as follows:

- 12 Light Field ambulance
- 15 Field Ambulance
- 12 Field Hygiene Section
- 12 Field Dressing Station

Medical officers were directly attached to the various battalions and regiments. The regimental medical officer worked with the regimental padre, who was a member of the Canadian Chaplain Service. The division also employed a dentist, who was a member of the Canadian Dental Corps.

Royal Canadian Ordnance Corps

The Ordnance Corps was responsible for the provisioning, storage, and distribution of various materials. It commanded the following sub-units:

- 4th Armoured Divisional Ordnance Field Park (OFP)
- Div. Sec. 4th Division Ordnance Sub-Park
- 4th Division OFP
- 4 Mobile Laundry and Bath Unit
- 7 Canadian Salvage unit

Royal Canadian Electrical and Mechanical Engineers

The RCEME engineering maintenance service, under the Commander, Royal (Canadian) Electrical and Mechanical Engineers (CRCEME), operated two second-line workshops (the 4th Brigade Workshop and the 10th Brigade Workshop) as well as a number of first-line mobile repair units (known as Light Aid Detachments or LADs) in every unit. The following LADs were embedded in the 4th Division:

- 29 CARR   No. 42
- 15 RCA   No. 44
- 23 RCA   No. 104
- 5 ATR RCA No. 45
- 8 LAA RCA No. 8 LAA
- RCE Fd Pk   No. 46
- RCCS Div.   No. 49
- LSR   No. 47
- 21 CAR   No. 75
- 22 CAR   No. 84
- 28 CAR   No. 41

- 10 Brig HQ   No. 48
- 4 Brig HQ   DADEME

Administrative troops

The administrative tasks at the various headquarters of the division, brigades, and regiments were performed by members of the Corps of Military Staff Clerks (CMSC). This corps was staffed for the most part by older men and those with infirmities that rendered them unfit for active service. Each regiment also had a Paymaster of the Royal Canadian Army Pay Corps (RCAPC) responsible for paying the troops.

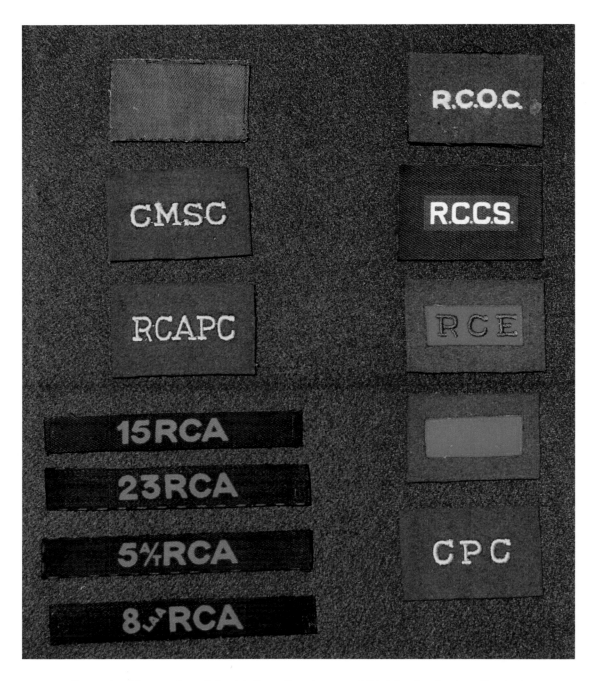

Some shoulder patches of the 4th Canadian Armoured Division (author's collection).

Patches of the 1st Canadian Army and the 2nd Canadian Corps. The patch at bottom left belongs to the Prince Edward Island Light Horse, the Defence and Employment Company of II Canadian Corps (author's collection).

Appendix III: War monuments in and near Steenbergen

The following list describes the monuments related to the liberation of Welberg and Steenbergen:

- The first monument to the Canadians who gave their lives in battle was officially unveiled in Moerstraten on 26 August 1945. It is located outside the built-up area, on Moerstraatsebaan in the direction of Bergen op Zoom. The monument marks the spot where the soldiers were buried before their mortal remains were moved to Bergen op Zoom.

- In 1947, a memorial plaque was unveiled on the wall of the town hall in Nieuw-Vossemeer. The street was renamed "Majoor Burkestraat" [Major Burke Street].

- In 1948, the dike connecting the Boomdijk and the Groenedijk was rechristened "Canadezenweg" (Canadians Road).

- Shortly after the war, a cross was erected at the end of the Glymesdijk to commemorate the war victims of Halsteren and Lepelstraat. The cross was located close to the spot where Rini

For many years after the war, a memorial was erected on the market square each year on Remembrance Day (collection P. Adriaansen).

Elling was shot and killed by the Germans. Rini had gone to the Glymes lock with a few O.D. friends on either 1 or 2 November. When they found themselves in a gun battle with the Germans, Rini covered the retreat of his comrades and was probably captured. He was shot in the back of the neck. The cross was later moved to a spot on the dike.

- On May 5th, 1955, the people of Welberg participated in a large-scale commemoration ceremony. A special church service was held in memory of all of Welberg's war victims, including those who perished in the Dutch East Indies. On that occasion, the section of Wipstraat located in the centre of Welberg was renamed Kapelaan Kockstraat (after the murdered curate).

- In 1958, a monument was unveiled in Steenbergen on Kerkplein (F5, Map IV). To this day, the annual Remembrance Day ceremony takes place there on May 4th.

- In 1985, a monument was unveiled in Dinteloord to commemorate the bombardment and the liberation.

- In 1994, a bronze plaque of the South Alberta Regiment was erected at the cemetery of Steenbergen. The plaque was donated by the veterans' association of the South Albertas.

- In 2003, a group of Welberg residents unveiled a war monument in the form of a church bell (also known as the "Liberation Monument") on Canadezenweg. The bell is solemnly rung every year on May 4th (the Dutch Remembrance Day) and 5th (Liberation Day), and whenever veterans visit the area. In late 2004, a bronze plaque listing the names of the Welberg war victims was added to the monument and a bronze shield of the Algonquin Regiment, donated by the Algonquin veterans' association, was mounted on the bell frame.

The war monument on Canadezenweg (author's collection).

Appendix IV: Canadian casualties in the battles of Welberg and Steenbergen

The lists below provide information about Canadian servicemen who lost their lives or were wounded in the area. The regimental abbreviations used are explained in Appendix I.

During the period from 29 October to 5 November 1944, 57 Canadian soldiers were killed in the Steenbergen area. A further 125 men were wounded (suffering injuries severe enough to prevent them from remaining on active duty with their units). Twenty-seven members of the Algonquin Regiment were taken prisoner. The total number of casualties was around 200 men.

Immediately after the liberation, a number of victims lay buried in field graves around Welberg and Steenbergen. Between three and seven field graves were located at the entrance to the Bogers farm along the Welbergsedijk (oral sources could not agree on the number). It is certain, however, that Sergeant Honey and Gunner Riley were among those buried there. They were crew members of the 5th Anti-Tank Regiment RCA artillery piece that was destroyed. They were buried on 4 November by members of the Regiment. The mortal remains of Private W.B. Cook of the Algonquin Regiment lay in the same location. One of the Canadian casualties was not found until several days after the liberation, in the fields near the Panhoef farm. The four Algonquins killed in the centre of Welberg during the night of 31 October / 1 November were buried in field graves on Hoogstraat. Soon afterwards, the remains of all Canadian victims were moved to Bergen op Zoom to a temporary location on Plein (Square) XIII. They were subsequently reburied in the Commonwealth War Cemetery in Bergen op Zoom.

Rank	Name	Regiment	Hometown	Date of death
Guardsman	J.D. Stronach	21 CAR (GGFG)	Carleton Place, ON	29 Oct. 1944
Guardsman	R.P. Tremblay	21 CAR (GGFG)	Ottawa, ON	29 Oct. 1944
Guardsman	R.R. Burns	21 CAR (GGFG)	Ottawa, ON	29 Oct. 1944
Guardsman	L.R. Kirker	21 CAR (GGFG)	Brinston, ON	29 Oct. 1944
Guardsman	V.J. Gardipee	21 CAR (GGFG)	Norwood Grove, MB	29 Oct. 1944
Private	E.R. Binch	LSR	Thornloe, ON	30 Oct. 1944
Lieutenant	F.B. Morrison	22 CAR (CGG)	Montreal, QC	31 Oct. 1944
Sergeant	J.R. Martin	22 CAR (CGG)	Foster, QC	31 Oct. 1944
Sergeant	J.W. Kearney	22 CAR (CGG)	Westmount, QC	31 Oct. 1944
Guardsman	B.L. Bendal	22 CAR (CGG)	Woodstock, ON	31 Oct. 1944
Guardsman	M.R.J. Graham	22 CAR (CGG)	St-Jean, QC	31 Oct. 1944
Private	J.E. Graham	LSR	Toronto, ON	31 Oct. 1944
Gunner	A.W. Curphey*	19 AFR RCA	Toronto, ON	01 Nov. 1944
Private	H.R. Prescott	AlgR	Picton, ON	01 Nov. 1944
Private	J. Prysiaznuk	AlgR	Emerson, MB	01 Nov. 1944
Private	J.P. Lone	AlgR	?	01 Nov. 1944
Private	J.W. Auld	AlgR	O'Leary Station, PE	01 Nov. 1944
Private	C.W. Hodgson	AlgR	Brampton, ON	02 Nov. 1944
Private	G.F. Phillips	AlgR	Toronto, ON	02 Nov. 1944
Private	J.P. Therrien	AlgR	St-Norbert, QC	02 Nov. 1944
Private	C.E. Judson	L&W	Sarnia, ON	02 Nov. 1944
Lance Corporal	F.J.H. Melanson	L&W	Val Albert, ON	02 Nov. 1944

Rank	Name	Regiment	Hometown	Date of death
Lance Corporal	R.S. Waterhouse	L&W	Sydney, NS	02 Nov. 1944
Private	N.A. Webb	L&W	Toronto, ON	02 Nov. 1944
Sergeant	M.R. Koll	5 A/T RCA	?	03 Nov. 1944
Lance Sergeant	H.A. Honey	5 A/T RCA	Dewberry, AB	03 Nov. 1944
Bombardier	R.M. Desjardins	5 A/T RCA	Windsor, ON	03 Nov. 1944
Lance Bombardier	D.L. Minion	5 A/R RCA	Lethbridge, AB	03 Nov. 1944
Gunner	C.J. Horner	5 A/T RCA	Woodside, NS	03 Nov. 1944
Gunner	A.S. McLelland	5 A/T RCA	New Victoria, NS	03 Nov. 1944
Gunner	G.W.H. Riley	5 A/T RCA	Newport Station, NS	03 Nov. 1944
Gunner	N. Rodgers	5 A/T RCA	Handsworth, SK	03 Nov. 1944
Gunner	S. Scott	5 A/T RCA	Spear Hill, MB	03 Nov. 1944
Gunner	H.B. Gunnarsen	5 A/T RCA	?	03 Nov. 1944
Gunner	D.E. Obre	5 A/T RCA	Moosomin, SK	03 Nov. 1944
Sapper	I.T. Davidson	9 FS RCE	Toronto, ON	03 Nov. 1944
Sergeant	C.C. Irwin	AlgR	Fort William, ON	03 Nov. 1944
Private	E.D. Hamilton	AlgR	?	03 Nov. 1944
Private	F.E. Foster	AlgR	?	03 Nov. 1944
Private	L.P. Smith	AlgR	?	03 Nov. 1944
Corporal	H.E. Allemang	AlgR	Lowbanks, ON	03 Nov. 1944
Corporal	R.D. Oliver	AlgR	Brantford, ON	03 Nov. 1944
Corporal	R.L. Frain	AlgR	London, ON	03 Nov. 1944
Private	W.B. Cook	AlgR	East Chester, NS	03 Nov. 1944
Private	E. Agnew	L&W	Moncton, NB	03 Nov. 1944
Private	R. Stever	L&W	?	03 Nov. 1944
Private	R.J. Needham	L&W	Hamilton, ON	03 Nov. 1944
Private	A. Roy	L&W	St-Nérée, QC	03 Nov. 1944
Private	D.H. Hiebert	LSR	Kleefeld, MB	03 Nov. 1944
Captain	J.S. Prugh	ASHofC	Hamilton, ON	04 Nov. 1944
Private	R.D. McPherson	ASHofC	Amherst, NS	04 Nov. 1944
Private	W.L. Thistle	L&W	Toronto, ON	04 Nov. 1944
Lieutenant	D.D. Stark	LSR	Winnipeg, MB	04 Nov. 1944
Private	M.E. Livingstone	L&W	Murray Harbour, PE	06 Nov. 1944
Gunner	E.J. Patterson	19 AFR RCA	Guelph, ON	07 Nov. 1944
Bombardier	H.C. Wetherup	19 AFR RCA	?	07 Nov. 1944
Sapper	H.C. Pettit	8 FS RCE	Toronto, ON	09 Nov. 1944

The mortal remains of A.W. Curphey have never been found.

The above list was compiled based on information from the regimental histories listed in the "Sources consulted" section on p.131 and verified against the list of the Commonwealth War Grave Commission consulted at http://www.cwgc.org/

The wounded

Rank	Name	Regiment	Date wounded
Guardsman	Draper	21 CAR (GGFG)	29 Oct. 1944
Guardsman	Maloney	21 CAR (GGFG)	29 Oct. 1944
Sergeant	Slater	21 CAR (GGFG)	29 Oct. 1944
Sergeant	B.C. Simmons	22 CAR (CGG)	29 Oct. 1944
Guardsman	Walker	22 CAR (CGG)	29 Oct. 1944
Guardsman	Walton	22 CAR (CGG)	29 Oct. 1944
Sergeant	Ketcheson	21 CAR (GGFG)	30 Oct. 1944
Guardsman	Lavson	21 CAR (GGFG)	30 Oct. 1944
Guardsman	Lewis	21 CAR (GGFG)	30 Oct. 1944
Lance Corporal	McKillop	21 CAR (GGFG)	30 Oct. 1944
Guardsman	St. Eloi	21 CAR (GGFG)	30 Oct. 1944
Guardsman	Westman	21 CAR (GGFG)	30 Oct. 1944
Guardsman	Wheeler	21 CAR (GGFG)	30 Oct. 1944
Private	E. Elliot	LSR	30 Oct. 1944
Lieutenant	W.E. Sills	23 FR (S-P) RCA	31 Oct. 1944
Lieutenant	F.N. Zimmerman	8 FS RCE	31 Oct. 1944
Private	S.F. Lucki	ASHofC	31 Oct. 1944
Private	W.R. Laurnitus	ASHofC	31 Oct. 1944
Corporal	D.S. Robertson	LSR	31 Oct. 1944
Private	G.J. Thompson	LSR	31 Oct. 1944
Private	G.R. McKay	LSR	31 Oct. 1944
Private	H.P. Peletier	LSR	31 Oct. 1944
Corporal	J. Baryluk	LSR	31 Oct. 1944
Lance Corporal	P.E. Berg	LSR	31 Oct. 1944
Private	R. Brothers	LSR	31 Oct. 1944
Sergeant	S.D.C. Miller	LSR	31 Oct. 1944
Private	W.E. Greer	LSR	31 Oct. 1944
Captain	R.J. Roberts	19 AFR RCA	01 Nov. 1944
Private	A.J. Chart	AlgR	01 Nov. 1944
Private	B.P. Acorn	AlgR	01 Nov. 1944
Private	C.D. Burke	AlgR	01 Nov. 1944
Private	H.C. Sloggett	AlgR	01 Nov. 1944
Private	H.E. Prince	AlgR	01 Nov. 1944
Private	J. Head	AlgR	01 Nov. 1944
Major	J.S. McLeod	AlgR	01 Nov. 1944
Private	K.C. MacLeod	AlgR	01 Nov. 1944
Private	L.W. Bower	AlgR	01 Nov. 1944
Lieutenant	R.E.A. Beckett	AlgR	01 Nov. 1944
Sergeant	W.E. Eaton	AlgR	01 Nov. 1944
Private	J.A. Evans	ASHofC	01 Nov. 1944
Private	W. Bosomworth	ASHofC	01 Nov. 1944
Lance Corporal	E.H. Veinot	LSR	01 Nov. 1944
Private	G. Backus	LSR	01 Nov. 1944
Private	J.F. McDonald	LSR	01 Nov. 1944
Gunner	McGillivary	LSR	01 Nov. 1944

Rank	Name	Regiment	Date wounded
Private	P. Deschutter	LSR	01 Nov. 1944
Corporal	G.J. Smith	AlgR	02 Nov. 1944
Private	J.B. Carruthers	AlgR	02 Nov. 1944
Private	J.D. Cross	AlgR	02 Nov. 1944
Private	R. Robinson	ASHofC	02 Nov. 1944
Sergeant	A.F. Christie	L&W	02 Nov. 1944
Private	B. Robinson	L&W	02 Nov. 1944
Private	C.J. Siminowski	L&W	02 Nov. 1944
Lance Sergeant	C.R. Lewis	L&W	02 Nov. 1944
Private	E. Celester	L&W	02 Nov. 1944
Private	E. Chmielnicki	L&W	02 Nov. 1944
Private	E.H. Tilker	L&W	02 Nov. 1944
Private	E.H. Torborg	L&W	02 Nov. 1944
Private	E.P. Arnold	L&W	02 Nov. 1944
Private	F. Riffel	L&W	02 Nov. 1944
Private	G.F. Patterson	L&W	02 Nov. 1944
Private	G.K. Taylor	L&W	02 Nov. 1944
Private	H. Garten	L&W	02 Nov. 1944
Private	H. Mackey	L&W	02 Nov. 1944
Private	H.T.E. Houseman	L&W	02 Nov. 1944
Private	J.C. Gnot	L&W	02 Nov. 1944
Corporal	J.E. Erwin	L&W	02 Nov. 1944
Private	J.E. Lauzon	L&W	02 Nov. 1944
Lieutenant	J.H. Taylor	L&W	02 Nov. 1944
Private	J.J. Charron	L&W	02 Nov. 1944
Private	J.V. Aubin	L&W	02 Nov. 1944
Private	K.D. MacDonald	L&W	02 Nov. 1944
Private	L.G. Hawes	L&W	02 Nov. 1944
Private	L.O. Lachance	L&W	02 Nov. 1944
Lieutenant	P.B. Maddox	L&W	02 Nov. 1944
Private	R. Kitcher	L&W	02 Nov. 1944
Corporal	R. Pyke	L&W	02 Nov. 1944
Lance Corporal	R.A. Wilson	L&W	02 Nov. 1944
Private	R.H. Landry	L&W	02 Nov. 1944
Lance Corporal	W. Reynoldson	L&W	02 Nov. 1944
Private	W.R. Keitch	L&W	02 Nov. 1944
Gunner	A.E. Pinnell	L&W	03 Nov. 1944
A/Sergeant	J.A. Wright	5 A/T RCA	03 Nov. 1944
Lieutenant	J.C. Hooke	5 A/T RCA	03 Nov. 1944
Bombardier	P. O'Brien	5 A/T RCA	03 Nov. 1944
Lance Bombardier	R. Lumsden	5 A/T RCA	03 Nov. 1944
Gunner	T.S. Rompf	5 A/T RCA	03 Nov. 1944
Private	B.W. Wark	AlgR	03 Nov. 1944
Corporal	C. Bell	AlgR	03 Nov. 1944
Private	H.S. Oram	AlgR	03 Nov. 1944
Private	J.D. Richardson	AlgR	03 Nov. 1944

Rank	Name	Regiment	Date wounded
Private	J.E. Carrington	AlgR	03 Nov. 1944
Private	J.H. Henry	AlgR	03 Nov. 1944
Corporal	J.W. Callender	AlgR	03 Nov. 1944
Corporal	J.W. Snyder	AlgR	03 Nov. 1944
Private	P.F. Serran	AlgR	03 Nov. 1944
Private	R.H. Reeves	AlgR	03 Nov. 1944
Private	R.P. Johnson	AlgR	03 Nov. 1944
Private	T.H. Jennings	AlgR	03 Nov. 1944
Private	W.F. Erwin	AlgR	03 Nov. 1944
Private	W. Morrisseau	ASHofC	03 Nov. 1944
Private	C.G. Chapman	L&W	03 Nov. 1944
Private	E.P. Haley	L&W	03 Nov. 1944
Private	K.M. Morrow	L&W	03 Nov. 1944
Private	F.M. Lemke	LSR	03 Nov. 1944
Private	G.M. McLean	LSR	03 Nov. 1944
Private	N.L. Kiser	LSR	03 Nov. 1944
Private	D.A. Turner	AlgR	04 Nov. 1944
Private	H.J. Homer	AlgR	04 Nov. 1944
Private	J.H. McLeod	ASHofC	04 Nov. 1944
Private	J.P. Murray	ASHofC	04 Nov. 1944
Sergeant	R.J.H. Harrison	ASHofC	04 Nov. 1944
Private	W.B. Keating	ASHofC	04 Nov. 1944
Private	C.G. Ollman	L&W	04 Nov. 1944
C.S.M.	C.M. Britton	L&W	04 Nov. 1944
Private	J.A. Robinson	L&W	04 Nov. 1944
Private	J.W. Meridith	L&W	04 Nov. 1944
Private	N.D. Blais	L&W	04 Nov. 1944
Private	J. Burger	LSR	04 Nov. 1944
Lieutenant	Brady	28 CAR (BCR)	07 Nov. 1944
Sapper	G.W. Glenn	8 FS RCE	unknown
Sapper	H.H. Hall	8 FS RCE	unknown
Sapper	J.H. Cliffe	8 FS RCE	unknown
Sapper	S.C. Masiowski	8 FS RCE	unknown
Sapper	B.R. McInnes	9 FS RCE	unknown

(*This list was compiled on the basis of information from the regimental histories listed in the section "Sources consulted." The list may contain names of persons who received their injuries from causes other than war-related activities.*)

"He, too, died for his country." Drawing of a German field grave at Visberg just south of Kruisland (collection L. Tholhuijsen, Kruisland).

Appendix V: Germans casualties in the battle of Steenbergen

The list below was compiled by J. Van Doorn [33]. The historical records consulted mention a total of 23 graves. Twenty of those men have been identified. No information is available regarding the number of missing and wounded. The number of Germans taken prisoner by the Canadians is estimated at between 40 and 50. Total German losses, including wounded and those taken prisoner, were probably around 150.

Known German field graves were located behind the Witkruis farm, and two bodies were found on Welbergsedijk near the intersection with Cromwielswegje. Others were located on Oudlandsestraat near the entrance to the Panhoef farm, in front of a small house on Koolbaantje, and in the yard of the Welberg presbytery. Another German field grave was situated on the corner of Westlandse Langeweg and Doornedijkje. Two German bodies were seen in a wheelbarrow on Welbergsedijk near Louis Raaijmakers' house, but it is not known where they were buried. A mass grave was dug on Krommeweg to accommodate the bodies of the Germans killed in action. A total of 12 German victims were buried there. In the fifties, their remains were moved to the German war cemetery in IJsselstein.

Rank	Name	Regiment	Date of death
	H. Bester	E. u. A. Regt. Hermann Göring	29 Oct. 1944
Gefreiter	H. Tautz	Gren. Regt. 937	29 Oct. 1944
	E. Oehl	XIVII Armee Korps	30 Oct. 1944
Gefreiter	P. Steffen	6. Fallschirmjäger Regt.	31 Oct. 1944
Jäger	G. Wieczorek	6. Fallschirmjäger Regt.	31 Oct. 1944
Oberjäger	E. Hinterser	6. Fallschirmjäger Regt.	31 Oct. 1944
	F. Doerr	E. u. A. Regt. Hermann Göring	31 Oct. 1944
Gefreiter	L. Deininger	E. u. A. Regt. Hermann Göring	31 Oct. 1944
Gefreiter	W. Weber	6. Fallschirmjaeger Regt.	01 Nov. 1944
Jäger	H. Schilling	E. u. A. Regt. Hermann Göring	Nov. 1944
Grenadier	W. Ebert	E. u. A. Regt. Hermann Göring	01 Nov. 1944
Schutze	G. E.W. Buse	E. u. A. Regt. Hermann Göring	01 Nov. 1944
Unteroffizier	H. Lindauer	2. Fallschirmjäger Regt.	01 Nov. 1944
Unteroffizier	K. K. Dietze	Gren. Regt. 937	02 Nov. 1944
Unteroffizier	H. Dechsel	Flieger Regiment 52 / 53	02 Nov. 1944
	O. Bilinski	E. u. A. Regt. Hermann Göring	02 Nov. 1944
Oberjäger	H. Huebener	6. Fallschirmjäger Regt.	03 Nov. 1944
Gefreiter	W. Manz	6. Fallschirmjäger Regt.	03 Nov. 1944
Gefreiter	K.H. Seufzer	Gren. Regt. 937	03 Nov. 1944
Oberjäger	J. Wirtz	6. Fallschirmjäger Regt.	03 Nov. 1944

Note: *Gefreiter* = Lance Corporal; *Schutze* = Private (Rifleman); *Jäger* = Private (Paratroopers); *Oberjäger* = Private First Class (Paratroopers); *Unteroffizier* = Sergeant; *Grenadier* = Private

Appendix VI: Decorations awarded to Canadian soldiers in the battle of Steenbergen

A number of distinguished military decorations were awarded to Canadian soldiers for bravery during the battle of Steenbergen.

Rank	Name	Regiment	Decoration	Date	Sector
Major	**Amy, E.A.C.**	22 CAR (CGG)	Distinguished Service Order	31 Oct. 1944	Bridgehead over the Oudlandse Watergang
S.Q.M.	**Brown, C.W.**	21 CAR (GGFG)	Bronzen Leeuw[19]	29 Oct. 1944	Halsters Laag
Captain	**Cameron, J.A.**	21 CAR (GGFG)	Ridder in the orde van Oranje Nassau met zwaarden[20]	29 Oct. 1944	Halsters Laag
Lance Corporal	**Dunn, A.J.**	21 CAR (GGFG)	Bronzen Leeuw	29 Oct. 1944	Halsters Laag
L/Sergeant	**Honey, H.A.**	5 A/T RCA	Mention in Despatch[21]	03 Nov. 1944	Welberg
Lieutenant	**Hooke, J.C.**	5 A/T RCA	Military Cross	03 Nov. 1944	Welbergsedijk
Lieutenant	**Liddell, K.C.**	21 CAR (GGFG)	Militaire Willems Orde[22]	29 Oct. 1944	Halsters Laag
Private	**Richard, F.J.**	LSR	Distinguished Conduct Medal	31 Oct. 1944	Bridgehead at the Witte Ruiter
Major	**Smith, E.M.**	21 CAR (GGFG)	Distinguished Service Order	29 Oct. 1944	Halsters Laag
Private	**Taylor, G.K.**	L&W	Military Medal	11 Mar. 1944	Tank wall Oudlandsestraat

The following section presents the citations that accompanied the decorations, reproduced in full from *Courage & Service, Second World War Awards to Canadians* [29].

---

[19] *Bronzen Leeuw*: a high Royal Dutch award intended for servicemen who have shown extreme bravery and leadership in battle favouring the Netherlands.

[20] *Ridder in the orde van Oranje Nassau met zwaarden*: the Order of Orange-Nassau (military version) was bestowed upon both members of the Dutch military and members of foreign services who helped liberate the Netherlands from the German occupation.

[21] MiDs may have been awarded to other soldiers during this episode. At the time of writing, this was the only one the author was aware of.

[22] *Militaire Willems Orde*: Military Order of William, a high military decoration awarded for bravery.

AMY, Edward Alfred Charles, Major, MC - Distinguished Service Order - Armour (22 Canadian Armoured Regiment) - awarded as per Canada Gazette and CARO/5283, both dated 20 January 1945. Recommended for immediate award, 18 November 1944; document with Headquarters, 4 Canadian Armoured Brigade, 22-23 November 1944 (supported by Brigadier R.W. Moncel); with Headquarters, 4 Canadian Armoured Division, 24-27 November 1944 (supported by Major General J.C. Jefferson, Acting General Officer Commanding); with Headquarters, 2 Canadian Corps, 28 November to 1 December 1944 (supported by Major General T.G. Rennie, Temporary Corps Commander); with Headquarters, First Canadian Army, 3-9 December 1944 (supported by General H.D.G. Crerar); final approval by Field Marshal B.L. Montgomery, Commander-in-Chief, 21 Army Group.

On 31 October 1944, No.1 Squadron, 22 Canadian Armoured Regiment commanded by Major Amy, with under his command one company of the Lake Superior Regiment (Motor) and a small party of Royal Canadian Engineers, was ordered to establish and maintain a bridgehead over the drainage canal and anti-tank ditch north of Moerstraten (Map Reference 6432, Sheet 4) on the main highway to Steenbergen. At 1900 hours, preceded by an artillery barrage, the Lake Superior Regiment (Motor) company crossed the river in assault boats and seized the bridgehead. The engineers bridged the obstacle and shortly before the first light of the next day Major Amy put two troops of tanks, a section of three reconnaissance tanks and his own tank across the bridge where they consolidated the position with the infantry. At daybreak the enemy counter-attacked with infantry armed with anti-tank projectors, two self-propelled guns and exceedingly heavy artillery and mortar fire. The small bridgehead force suffered heavy casualties from the shell fire. Major Amy, realizing the importance of keeping the bridgehead intact, immediately visited each of his tanks and encouraged the crews. He also visited many of the infantry positions to hearten the men, helping them to withstand the shelling by his own high spirits and apparent disregard for personal danger. The attack was beaten off successfully but the enemy continued to shell and mortar the position heavily throughout the remainder of the day. Major Amy directed much of the counter-battery work through his Forward Observation Officer, and in several cases personally flash-spotted the enemy guns. He made the rounds of the bridgehead several more times during the day, always cheerful and confident and inspiring his officers and men. At dusk that evening the Algonquin regiment passed through the bridgehead and launched its attack on Steenbergen. Major Amy, by his example and determination to maintain the bridgehead in a place where the soggy nature of the ground prevented his tanks from deploying to defend the position, enabled 10 Canadian Infantry Brigade to pass through and launch their attack which destroyed German resistance in the Steenbergen area.

BROWN, Claude William, Warrant Officer Class II (Squadron Sergeant-Major) (C.40012) - Bronze Lion (Holland) - Armour (21 Canadian Armoured Regiment, the Governor General's Foot Guards) - awarded as per Canada Gazette dated 22 December 1945 and CARO/6291 dated 24 December 1945. Recommended by Lieutenant Colonel E.M. Smith, Commanding Officer, 21 Canadian Armoured Regiment (Governor General's Foot Guards); supported by Lieutenant Colonel G.D. de Salaberry Wotherspoon, Acting Officer Commanding 4 Canadian Armoured Brigade which had the form 26-27 August 1945; supported by Brigadier C.M. Drury, Acting General Officer Commanding 4 Canadian Armoured Division; with Headquarters, Canadian

Forces in the Netherlands, 6-26 September 1945 when signed off by Lieutenant-General G.G. Simonds.

On 21 October 1944 during the campaign to clear the enemy from south of the Maas River, the regiment found itself in front line contact north of Putte without infantry support. Sergeant-Major Brown was given the responsibility of defending the tanks against enemy infiltration tactics. Although exposed to direct enemy fire, this Warrant Officer carried out a reconnaissance of the regiment's entire front with complete disregard for his personal safety. After dark, Bren gun teams which he had personally picked and trained from the regiment's supply echelon clerks, drivers and batmen for just such an emergency as this, were brought forward and he led them to the positions which he had previously chosen. Throughout the night in the face of constant enemy harassing machine gun fire, this Warrant Officer paid continual visits to his outposts of improvised infantry, and by his example of fearlessness and cheerfulness while under enemy fire, inspired his inexperienced command with the courage of old campaigners. At least one German infiltration attempt was beaten off and two enemy killed.

Another instance of Sergeant-Major Brown's coolness under fire took place on 29 October 1944. The regiment liberated the towns of Heerle and Moerstraaten and fought to the main road between Bergen op Zoom and Steenbergen. Petrol and ammunition were practically exhausted on this long advance, so this Warrant Officer led a supply convoy forward to replenish the tanks. On returning to Heerle, the convoy of empty vehicle was attacked by an enemy patrol with small arms. Without hesitation, Sergeant-Major Brown engaged the enemy with the Bren gun mounted on top of his scout car. His fire was so effective that the enemy withdrew and the convoy was able to complete its return to Heerle. This Warrant Officer's personal initiative, courage and leadership have served as a constant example to all ranks of the regiment and have contributed materially to the success of the regiment as a fighting unit during the operations in Holland.

CAMERON, John Allan, Captain - Knight Officer of the Order of Orange-Nassau (with Swords) (Holland) - Service Corps - awarded as per Canada Gazette dated 22 December 1945 and CARO/6291 dated 24 December 1945. Recommendation initiated 24 August 1945; with Headquarters First Canadian Army, 6-26 September 1945.

Captain John Allan Cameron was appointed Staff Captain 10 Canadian Infantry Brigade in September 1944 and has continued in this appointment to date. During the period of fighting for the liberation of the Bergen op Zoom and Steenbergen area in Holland, Captain Cameron was charged with the responsibility of maintaining the armoured and infantry units of his brigade. This included all types of supplies and the accurate forecast of administrative requirements for operations. These tasks were carried out in a most practical and efficient manner. During the winter of 1944-45, as 10 Canadian Infantry Brigade was guarding a part of the Meuse River, the administrative details for raids and special patrols into enemy-held territory taxed the ingenuity and resourcefulness of the administrative staff. These problems, however, were always answered by Captain Cameron with the supplies or equipment on the ground in time. During the 1945 spring campaign through Holland, the administrative staff were confronted with giving the maximum assistance to the civilian authorities couples with the normal battle maintenance of a rapid advance. Both of these tasks were successfully accomplished. It has been due in no small measure to the efforts of Captain Cameron, his initiative, enthusiasm and drive that the brigade's administrative plan throughout the operations in Holland has always been successful.

DUNN, Allan James, Lance Corporal (C.58524) - Bronze Lion (Netherlands) - Armour (21 Canadian Armoured Regiment, Governor General's Foot Guards) - awarded as per Canada Gazette dated 22 December 1945 and CARO/6291 dated 24 December 1945. Recommended by Lieutenant Colonel E.M. Smith, Commanding Officer, 21 Canadian Armoured Regiment; document with Headquarters, 4 Canadian Armoured Brigade, 26-27 August 1945 where approved by Lieutenant Colonel G.D. de Salaberry Wotherspoon, Acting Officer Commanding; duly passed by Brigadier C.M. Drury, Acting General Officer Commanding, 4 Canadian Armoured Division; with Headquarters, Canadian Forces in the Netherlands, 6-26 September 1945 when signed off by Lieutenant-General G.G. Simonds.

Lance Corporal Dunn has been a member of the regiment throughout the entire campaign in Holland. His actions at all times have been outstanding and his courage and leadership beyond question. On 29 October 1944 the regiment was engaged in a bitter struggle with the enemy as an attempt was made to cut the enemy main retreat road from Bergen op Zoom to Steenbergen. The ground was almost impassable to tanks and in the heavy going many bogged down and were subjected to intense enemy shelling, mortaring and anti-tank fire which continually swept the open fields. Lance Corporal Dunn was a crew commander of the tank on the extreme right of the regimental advance and, as such, was responsible for right flank protection during the move across the open fire-swept country. When he was approximately half-way towards the objective his tank suddenly bogged down. With complete disregard for his own personal safety and realizing the importance of his particular task, Lance Corporal Dunn continued to fight his tank and neutralize enemy fire on the regimental right flank. An enemy anti-tank gun attempted to bring fire down, but quickly spotting the position, Lance Corporal Dunn engaged and brought such effective fire to bear that the enemy gun was knocked out. The regiment continued its dash forward, with the right flank protected by the effective fire from Lance Corporal Dunn's tank. Lance Corporal Dunn remained with his tank during the night and towards dawn a cry was heard for help. Realizing that a comrade was lying wounded near one of the knocked out tanks, and heedless of the enemy fire, he led a party towards the area from which the cry had come. As the party moved forward they were suddenly pinned to the ground by enemy machine gun fire which swept over the area. Lance Corporal Dunn shouted to his party to give him cover and crawled forward towards his wounded comrade. As he wormed his way forward he found a Sergeant from one of the knocked out tanks lying in a slit trench severely wounded. Unable to move the man, Lance Corporal Dunn administered first aid; then crawling back to where he had left the party, he sent a message back to the regiment. He himself returned and stayed with the Sergeant until the wounded man was evacuated. This display of courage and resourcefulness displayed by this Non-Commissioned Officer was undoubtedly responsible for the saving of the life of this Sergeant. His utter lack of fear has been a source of inspiration at all times to the men under his command. His actions, leadership and courage in this and many other instances played a large part in the success attained by the regiment in Holland.

HONEY, Hedley Arthur, Lance Sergeant – Mention in Despatch - RCA (5th Canadian Anti-Tank Regiment)

[The citation could not be located, but below is the text of the letter Lieutenant J.C. Hooke (below) wrote to Lance Sergeant Honey's family[23]:]

"Two nights ago, the troop was ordered forward to help some of our own infantry, who held one end of a little Dutch village and who were threatened by counter attack by enemy tanks and infantry. The guns were put into position and until morning, the boys were subjected to heavy shelling from the Germans. During the hours before first light, we heard enemy tanks moving around only a couple of hundred yards away, and we could hear the Germans giving orders. At first light, the enemy tanks and infantry started to attack, and Hedley moved his gun so that he could better view their attack. Eventually, one of the enemy tanks showed itself, as Hedley's gunner could not identify the target in the trees where it was. Hedley himself took over the job and fired the first round, which killed the enemy tank. The enemy infantry continued to come in and so Hedley manned his machine gun and caused them to halt, then start to withdraw, and he continued to fire at them. The enemy broke in disorder and fled. During the whole of the attack and subsequent retreat, there was no one except Hedley and his crew who helped him in his task. Had it not been for his courage, coolness and resourcefulness, the whole of the infantry position would have been overrun, and the fighting in that sector of the past week would have been in vain. It is almost solely due to Hedley that our own boys were able to advance a further 10 miles in our sector in the next 24 hours.

Hedley was killed that morning, firing his gun to the end."

HOOKE, John Christopher, Lieutenant - Military Cross - RCA (5 Canadian Anti-Tank Regiment) - awarded as per Canada Gazette dated 10 February 1945 and CARO/5352 of that date. Recommended for immediate award, 18 November 1944; document at Brigade Headquarters level, 10 November to 4 December 1944; with Headquarters, 4 Canadian Armoured Division, 6-10 December 1944; with Headquarters, 1 British Corps, 10-15 December 1944; with Army Headquarters, 16 December 1944 to 2 January 1945.

On 2 November Lieutenant Hooke was in command of a troop of M-10 17-Pounders which was in support of "D" Company, the Algonquin Regiment. The company was ordered to capture the eastern portion of the village of Welberg (Map Reference 6436 Holland 1:25,000 sheet 15 NE) to enable other troops to pass through and capture Steenbergen 6337. The company reached its objective and Lieutenant Hooke, on foot under intense mortar and shell fire, led each one of his guns into position. During the night 2/3 November he moved from gun to gun, carefully briefing the men as well as altering the position of two guns to meet the threat of enemy self-propelled guns which could be heard moving into position on the western edge of the village. At first light, German infantry supported by two self-propelled guns counter-attacked and drove the infantry

---

[23] Quoted from an article in the Lloydminster Meridian Booster on 25 September 2006, accessed on-line at http://www.meridianbooster.com/ on 1August 2010.

133

behind Lieutenant Hooke's forward gun. Under this officer's personal supervision this gun was kept in action, destroying one enemy self-propelled gun and broke up the enemy infantry attack with its .5 machine gun fire. The infantry was able to come forward and regain its hold on the village from which the successful attack on Steenbergen was launched. There can be no doubt that Lieutenant Hooke's courage and coolness under fire and intrepid handling of his 17-Pounders were responsible for the capture and retention of the village.

LIDDELL, Kenneth Cecil, Lieutenant - Militaire Willems Orde, Degree of Knight of the Fourth Class (Netherlands) - Armour (21 Canadian Armoured Regiment [Governor General's Foot Guards]) - awarded as per Canada Gazette dated 22 December 1945 and CARO/6291 dated 24 December 1945. Recommended by Lieutenant Colonel E.M. Smith, Commanding Officer, 21 Canadian Armoured Regiment (Governor General's Foot Guards); with Headquarters, 4 Canadian Armoured Brigade, 26-27 August 1945 when approved by Lieutenant Colonel G.D. de Salaberry Wotherspoon, Acting Officer Commanding 4 Canadian Armoured Brigade which held the document 22-28 August 1945; cleared by Brigadier C.M. Drury, Acting General Officer Commanding 4 Canadian Armoured Division; at Headquarters, Canadian Forces in the Netherlands, 6-26 September 1945 when signed off by Lieutenant-General G.G. Simonds.

On 29 October 1944, the 21 Canadian Armoured Regiment was ordered to move forward astride the railway line in the immediate vicinity of Heerle, Holland, and to then attack and capture the town of Moerstraaten. Lieutenant Liddell was commanding a troop of 2 Squadron and was ordered to advance on the town of Heerle as lead troop and to lead the way through to the second objective, Moerstraaten. Under blistering enemy mortar, machine gun and anti-tank fire, this officer pressed the attack forward. Accurate anti-tank fire knocked out one of the four tanks but undaunted and fully realizing that speed was essential for the success of the attack, Lieutenant Liddell quickly pressed beyond the railway and continued to the west of the town. The speed and dash of the manoeuvre, despite the heavy direct shell fire, demoralized the enemy and, before they could recover, Lieutenant Liddell positioned the three tanks of the troop in fire positions from where his accurate fire accounted for two enemy armoured vehicles. The enemy attempted to retreat towards prepared defences on the second objective and quickly rallying his tanks, Lieutenant Liddell moved forward to attack Moerstraaten before the enemy could completely organize the defensive position. As the troop advanced this officer brought down heavy fire on the first two anti-tank guns of the enemy defences, demolishing both and killing five crew members. As the enemy fire thickened, a high explosive shell landed squarely on the back deck plate of the officer's tank and although the basket box was knocked off, the engine was undamaged. To press home the advantage already gained, Lieutenant Liddell moved forward straight into the centre of the town, spraying the houses with all the weapons and fire at his disposal. The Germans retreated in utter confusion to the outskirts of the town. On passing through the town and reaching a wooded area, Lieutenant Liddell discovered an enemy infantry force forming up to counter-attack. Realizing if this attack should be allowed to develop that the squadron advancing on Moerstraaten might be seriously endangered, this officer took up fire positions with his tanks. The enemy, under a protective artillery concentration, suddenly moved from the cover of the woods to counter-attack. An armour-piercing shell crashed into the second tank causing it to burst into flames. Alone and with no flank protection, Lieutenant Liddell engaged the advancing enemy and his fire was so effective that the counter-attack was broken up and the enemy again dispersed. This action enabled the squadron to move forward, capture the town and further exploit the success to cut the main highway and enemy line of retreat from Bergen op Zoom to Steenbergen. Coolness under heavy fire, courage, initiative and outstanding leadership in the face of tough enemy opposition was not only shown on this occasion but in many similar instances as Lieutenant Liddell fought with his troop. His ability to take the initiative at the opportune time, together with speed and dash in the attack, directly reflected on the crew and the ultimate success of many encounters.

RICHARD, Francis Joseph, Private (H.46459) - Distinguished Conduct Medal - Infantry (The Lake Superior Regiment [Motor]) - awarded as per Canada Gazette and CARO/5283, both dated 20 January 1945. Immediate award; originated by Lieutenant Colonel R.A. Keane on 7 November 1944; supported by Brigadier R.W. Moncel, Commanding 4 Canadian Armoured Brigade on 9 November 1944 and passed forward on 10 November 1944; endorsed by Major General H.W. Foster, General Officer Commanding, 4 Canadian Armoured Division on 11 November 1944 and passed forward on 13 November 1944; endorsed by Headquarters, 1 Canadian Corps on 24 November 1944 and passed forward on 28 November 1944; approved by General H.D.G. Crerar, General Officer Commanding-in-Chief, First Canadian Army on 16 November 1944 and passed forward on 4 December 1944; approved by Field Marshal B.L. Montgomery, Commander-in-Chief, 21 Army Group.

On 31 October 1944, during the advance of 4 Canadian Armoured Brigade towards Steenbergen (Map Reference 6337), "C" Company, Lake Superior Regiment (Motor), was ordered to secure a bridgehead over the stream at Map Reference 633353. The line of the stream was held in considerable strength, and the area where the crossing was to be made was under heavy and accurate fire from enemy SA, artillery and mortars. The assault was to be made with two platoons. On the right, the platoon to which Private Richard belonged was ordered to cross and secure a road junction at Map Reference 635357. The crossing was successfully made at 2300 hours, but during the approach to their objective, Private Richard's platoon came under heavy enemy defensive fire as a result of which both the Platoon Commander and the last remaining Non-Commissioned Officer became casualties. The platoon very quickly became disorganized and the advance came to a halt. At this point, and in spite of the enemy fire, Private Richard assumed command of the platoon, rallied it and led the men forward to their positions, where they dug in and prepared to hold the ground they had gained. When daylight came, the platoon came under observed fire from enemy small arms weapons, as well as almost continuous mortar and artillery fire. Despite the enemy fire, Private Richard retained complete control of the platoon going about from post to post encouraging his men and supervising the defence of the position until relieved at 1900 hours on 1 November 1944. The initiative, quick assumption of responsibility well above what might be reasonably expected of him, and the leadership displayed by Private Richard in the face of heavy enemy fire undoubtedly played a great part in the success of this operation. The bridgehead thus secured was subsequently used by 10 Canadian Infantry Brigade for their assault on the town of Steenbergen itself.

SMITH, Edward Marshall, Major (Acting Lieutenant Colonel) - Distinguished Service Order - Armour (21 Canadian Armoured Regiment [Governor General's Foot Guards]) - awarded as per Canada Gazette and CARO/5283, both dated 20 January 1945. Recommended for immediate award by Brigadier R.W. Moncel, Commander, 4 Canadian Armoured Brigade, on or about 5 November 1944; document with Headquarters, 4 Canadian Armoured Division, 6-13 November 1944 (supported by Major General H.W. Foster); with Headquarters, 1 British Corps, 24-28 November 1944; with Headquarters, First Canadian Army, until 4 December 1944, supported by General H.D.G. Crerar; final approval by Field Marshal B.L. Montgomery, Commander-in-Chief, 21 Army Group.

By the evening of 28 October 1944, 4 Canadian Armoured Division had fought its way up to the general line, Bergen op Zoom, Map Reference 605275, and the railway running east out of the town. 10 Canadian Infantry Brigade was held by stubborn enemy resistance at Bergen op Zoom itself. The leading elements of 4 Canadian Armoured Brigade had reached Vijfhoek, Map Reference 551285. The enemy position was greatly strengthened on the left by an array of obstacles and extensive mining. The right flank was flat open country with many ditches, and afforded excellent fields of fire. The ground itself was very soft and limited the manoeuvrability of tanks as well as being extensively mined. On the night of 28/29 October 1944, it was decided that on 29 October, 21 Canadian Armoured Regiment, under command of Lieutenant Colonel Smith, would try to work across country, bypassing the towns of Heerle and Hazelaar up to Moerstraten, then turn west and attempt to cut the main escape road running northeast from Bergen op Zoom to Steenbergen. The operation involved moving unsupported across ground which was known to be heavily mined and was treacherous in that only in certain places could tanks physically move, let alone fight. In addition, this area was under direct observation of a number of enemy self-propelled guns. However, it appeared that the operation had a reasonable chance to succeed provided that a route which would support an armoured regiment could be found over the marshy ground. The operation was commenced at 0830 hours on 29 October 1944. By 1200 hours, the leading elements of the regiment had reached Moerstraten and were coming under heavy observed fire. Several tanks had bogged down en route but by sheer persistence these had been recovered and got under way again. By 1600 hours the regiment was assembled around Moerstraten and had started on the task of finding a route to the west to its objective. By last light a route had been found and the regiment was positioned within 1,000 yards of the main road with patrols actually on the road. It was a bright night and observation and complete domination of the road by fire was possible. When fire was brought down to bear on any move on the road, it became apparent to the enemy that his position in Bergen op Zoom was now untenable and he was forced to withdraw using a route further to the west. Throughout this operation Lieutenant Colonel Smith displayed the greatest initiative and fortitude. Constantly under aimed fire, he personally directed the operation of his regiment, and it was only by his skill, perseverance and example that a route to this dominating position was discovered. The success of the regiment is a gauge of his efforts. His courage and devotion to duty under extremely difficult conditions are in keeping with the best of Canadian fighting traditions. There can be no doubt that the successful domination of this road by 21 Canadian Armoured Regiment contributed very largely to the capture of the town of Bergen op Zoom by 10 Canadian Infantry Brigade.

TAYLOR, Gordon Kendall, Private (B.138266) - Military Medal - Infantry (Lincoln and Welland Regiment) - awarded as per Canada Gazette dated 10 February 1945 and CARO/5352 of that date. Immediate award; so recommended on 23 November 1944; supported by Headquarters, 10 Canadian Infantry Brigade on 3 December 1944 and passed forward on 5 December 1944; supported by Headquarters, 4 Canadian Armoured Division on 6 December 1944 and passed forward on 10 December 1944; supported by Headquarters, 1 British Corps on 10 December 1944 and passed forward on 15 December 1944; approved by Army on 16 December 1944 and forward on 2 January 1945.

In Holland on the night 3/4 November 1944, The Lincoln and Welland Regiment was engaged in an attack north of Bergen op Zoom as part of the operation to seize Steenbergen. At approximately 2030 hours, 3 November 1944, while proceeding under intense enemy mortar and machine gun fire, Private Taylor was painfully wounded in the leg. Casualties had been heavy and the battalion's fighting strength was dangerously low with a consequent lowering of the morale of the remaining men. Realizing the vital need for every available man, Private Taylor continued to man his Bren gun until his company's objective had been taken. When the company had dug in, he continued to fight and on two occasions, despite the severe pain he was suffering, he crawled over open country to give assistance to wounded comrades. By the following morning he could no longer walk but he remained at his post until ordered by his Company Commander to go back for medical treatment. The courage and tenacity shown by Private Taylor went far beyond the call of normal duty and was a magnificent example to all ranks of his company and battalion.

Regimental histories and other publications

[1] *Warpath. The Story of the Algonquin Regiment, 1939–1945.* Maj. G.L. Cassidy (Toronto: Ryerson Press, 1948).

[2] *Einddoel Maas: De strijd in Zuidelijk Nederland tussen september en december 1944.* Jack Didden and Maarten Swarts (Weesp: De Gooise Uitgeverij, 1984).

[3] *XII Manitoba Dragoons: A Tribute, 1885-1991.* Bruce Tascona (Altona, MB: The Regiment, 1991).

[4] *July 1944 - May 1945: A Brief History of the 4th Canadian Armoured Brigade in Action.* Major G.M. Alexander, ed. (Mitcham, Surrey [UK]: West Brothers, 1945).

[5] *A Short History of the 10th Canadian Infantry Brigade*, Maj. R.A. Paterson (Hilversum: De Jong, 1945).

[6] *South Albertas: A Canadian Regiment at War.* Donald E. Graves (Toronto: Robin Brass Studio, 2004).

[7] *The Argyll and Sutherland Highlanders of Canada (Princess Louise's), 1928-1953.* Lt Col. H.M. Jackson (Montreal: The Regiment, 1953).

[8] *History of the Lincoln and Welland Regiment*, Major R.L. Rogers (n.p., 1954).

[9] *1st Bn. The New Brunswick Rangers*, Lt. P.R. Robinson (n.p., privately printed, n.d.).

[10] *The History of the 5th Canadian Anti Tank Regiment.* J.P. Claxton (n.p., 1945).

[11] *The History of the 23rd Field Regiment (SP) R.C.A., April 1942 to May 1945.* Lt L.N. Smith (St Catharines, ON: St. Catharines Standard, 1945)

[12] *The History of the Fifteenth Canadian Field Regiment: Royal Canadian Artillery: 1941 to 1945.* Capt. R.A. Spencer (New York: Elsevier, 1945)

[13] *In the Face of Danger: The History of the Lake Superior Regiment.* Lt. Col. G.F.G. Stanley (Port Arthur, ON: Lake Superior Scottish Regiment, 1960).

[14] *The Regimental History of the Governor General's Foot Guards.* A committee of the Guards (Ottawa: Mortimer, 1948).

[15] *History of the Canadian Grenadier Guards: 1760-1964.* Col. A. Fortescue Duguid (Montreal: Gazette Printing Co., 1965).

[16] *Green Route Up*. Lieutenant M.O. Rollefson, ed. (The Hague: Mouton, 1945).

[17] *Canada's Army in World War II : Badges and Histories of the Corps and Regiments*. F.R. Tripp (Toronto: Unitrade Press, c.1983).

[18] *The History of the 8th Canadian Light Anti-Aircraft Regiment, R.C.A.* Capt. W.S. Russell (Amersfoort, the Netherlands: 1945).

[19] *Canada's Craftsmen at 50*. Col. Murray Johnston (Bordon, ON: EME Officers' Fund, 1997).

[20] *Official History of the Canadian Army in the Second World War: Volume III. The Victory Campaign, The Operations in North-West Europe: 1944-1945*. Col. C.P. Stacey (Ottawa: Queen's Printer, 1966).

[21] *Kroniek van Steenbergen*, Liberation Issue 1994, vols 1 and 2, Con Slokkers (Private local newsletter)

[22] *Halsteren en Lepelstraat in de tweede wereldoorlog*, Halchterth Historical Society

[23] *Battery flashes of W.W.II : a thumb-nail sketch of Canadian artillery batteries during the 1939-1945 conflict*. D.W. Falconer (Victoria, B.C.: 1985).

[24] *The Canadian Soldier in World War II*. Jean Bouchery (Paris: Histoire & Collections, 2007).

[25] *The Gunners of Canada: The History of the Royal Regiment of Canadian Artillery*. Col. G.W.L. Nicholson (Toronto: McClelland & Stewart, 1972)

[26] Document produced by Mr P.C.M. van Wesel, Nispen

[27] *Die Löwen von Carentan. Das Fallschirmjäger-Regiment 6: 1943-1945*. Volker Griesser (n.p.: VS Books, 2007)

[28] *Dinteloord, Oorlogsherinneringen*, Gerard van Saarloos (n.p., privately printed, n.d.)

[29] *Courage & Service, Second World War Awards to Canadians*. John Blatherwick and Hugh Halliday (Ottawa: Service Publications, 2003).

[30] *Jaarboek 1998*, Steenbergen Historical Society.

[31] *Het vroegere Lepelstraat*, P. van Tilbeurgh (n.p., privately printed, n.d.).

[32] *History of the 7th Canadian Medium Regiment R.C.A. From 1st September, 1939 to 8th June, 1945. World War 2.* Capt. A.M. Lockwood with Major W. G. Ferguson & Major W. H. Gillespie (Toronto: Macmillan Company of Canada, 1945).

[33] *Operatie "Rebound": Bevrijding van de Westhoek, oktober / november 1944.* J. van Doorn (Willemstad, 1994).

[34] *Black Yesterdays: The Argylls' War.* R. L. Fraser (Hamilton, ON: Argyll Regimental Foundation, 1996).

Historical records

[35] War Diary, 10th Canadian Infantry Brigade, November 1944.

[36] War Diary, 4th Canadian Armoured Brigade, October 1944.

[37] Kriegstagebuch, 88. Armee Korps.

[38] War Diary, Lincoln and Welland Regiment, November 1944.

[39] War Diary, 19th (Army) Field Regiment RCA, November 1944.

[40] War Diary, 8th Field Squadron RCA, November 1944.

[41] Police Report No. 59, 5 March 1945.

[42] War Diary, 4th Canadian Armoured Division, November 1944.

[43] War Diary, 5th Anti-tank Regiment, November 1944.

[44] War Diary, Algonquin Regiment, November 1944.

Diaries /Memoirs

[45] Diary, Major Keith Stirling, written in POW camp OFLAG 79. Unpublished.

[46] *Peewees on Parade: Wartime Memories of a Young (and Small) Soldier.* John A. Galipeau and P. Whitehouse (Toronto: Robin Brass Studio, 2002).

[47] *Steel my Soldiers' Hearts.* Neil J. Stewart (Victoria, BC: Trafford Publishing, 2000).

[48] *The Warpath Days as Seen by Sgt. George L. Caya, M.M.* George Caya (n.p., privately printed, n.d.).

[49] *Those Army Days.* Larry Brown (n.p., privately printed, 1997).

Newspapers

[50] Steenbergse Courant, 24 November 1944 (liberation issue)

[51] Steenbergse Courant, 4 November 1969 (memorial issue)

[52] Hamilton Spectator, 22 November 1944 (article by Russ Munro)

[53] Hamilton Spectator, 23 January 1945.

Interviews

Name / Date interviewed	Date of birth / death	Address in 1944
Alma van Broekhoven–de Boevere 2004 – October 2007	27/10/1911-16/10/2007	Corneliusstraat
Adri "Ad" Helmons 13 December 2008	27/05/1933-	Koolbaantje
Jan Gladdines 17 January 2009	06/01/1929-	Krommeweg
Kees van Eekelen 17 January 2009	23/07/1931-	Witkruis
Anna Luykx-Geers 2 November 2008	03/06/1928-	Pomphoef
Tiny van der Heijden 10 November 2007	13/04/1932-19/12/2008	Oudlandsestraat
Lisa Augustijn-de Jong 6 February 2009	12/02/1931-	Oudlandsestraat
Helena Helmons-Iriks 15 March 2009	08/02/1930-	Welbergsedijk
Govert Helmons 15 March 2009	21/11/1925-	Koolbaantje
Janus Geers 8 April 2009	30/06/1930-	Welbergsedijk
Bart Gorissen 16 April 2009	12/08/1928-	Welbergsedijk
Frans Koolen 7 May 2009	21/09/1929-	Dwarsdijk
Riet Jonkers-van Hooijdonk 5 May 2010	05/02/1930-	Kinderbaantje

Appendix VIII: List of maps

No.	Description	Page
I	The advance of the 4th Canadian Armoured Division from Antwerp to Steenbergen in 1944. Copied from *Green Route Up* [16].	4
II	The Northern Front, October/November 1944	8
III	Modern map of Steenbergen/Welberg and surroundings (© Falkplan BV)	9
IV	Modern map of Steenbergen and Welberg (© Falkplan BV)	10
V	Canadian ordnance map showing the German defence line around Steenbergen.	16
VI	Fragment of a map from the regimental history of the Canadian Grenadier Guards with a diagram of the advance of the units of the 4th Armoured Brigade.	20
VII	The Battles for Welberg from *Warpath*	54
VIII	1944 Canadian ordnance map of Steenbergen and Welberg	59
IX	The same 1944 ordnance map with the names of a number of farms and families in the vicinity of Steenbergen	60

Index of names of persons
(The index covers p. 1-96 and does not incorporate the lists of names found in the appendices)

A

Adriaansen, family · 66, 79
Adriaansen, farmer · 64, 99
Alexander, Captain G.M. · 23, 24
Allemang, Corporal H.E. · 67
Allen, Major · 29
Amy, Major E.A.C. · 29, 30, 31
Arnot, Sergeant · 41
Atkinson · 34, 35
Atkinson, Major Don · 34
Atkinson, Major J.D. · 35, 45, 52
Augustijn, Henk · 65
Augustijn, Piet · 56

B

Baartmans · 37
Baartmans, Jan · 37, 38
Baartmans, Mijntje · 63
Baartmans, Mr · 96
Bachmeier, Private L. · 45
Backx, Mrs · 78
Barkman, Captain W.H. · 57
Bastiaansen · 90
Baylay, Major G.T. · 18
Beaulieu, Private R. · 45
Beckett, Lieutenant R.E. · 34, 35
Beleter, Mrs · 63
Bell, Corporal B.H. · 36
Bendal, Guardsman Brock · 31
Bernaards, Kees · 38
Bird, Private · 83
Blake, Private J.W. · 45
Bogers, farmer · 63, 81
Bokelaar, Mies · 79
Bowes, Private F.G. · 45
Bradburn, Lieutenant Colonel R.A. · 31, 52

Brady, Lieutenant · 77
Brisbois, Corporal W.J. · 45
Brooks, Private W.O. · 45
Brouwers, Rochus · 49
Brown, Private L. · 67
Brownlee, Private A.M. · 45
Buckingham, Private F.D. · 45
Buffin, Company Sergeant Major K.M. · 35
Burke, Captain · 83
Butcher, Private R.K. · 45
Buuron, Marijn · 53

C

Callander, Corporal J.W. · 56
Campbell, Sergeant G. · 62
Canavan, Lieutenant · 25
Carroll, Private B.C. · 44, 45
Cassidy, Major G.L. · 33, 35n, 42, 52, 56, 57, 62, 63, 66, 67, 68
Caya, Sergeant G.L. · 34, 43
Chambers, Private F. · 45
Chapman · 73
Chapman, Captain S.D. · 47
Chill, General Kurt · 3, 6, 8
Conrad, Corporal P.R. · 67
Costello, Sergeant G.T. · 45, 46, 47
Cox, Private W.E. · 45
Curphey, Gunner A.W. · 37, 43

D

Dawson, Major · 30
de Jong, family · 86
de Jong, Hylke · 84
de Jong, Lies · 87
de Jong, Marie · 86
de Jong, Mr · 22

De Weert, family · 44
De Weert, Mr · 56
Desjardin, Bombardier R.M. · 55
Dickie, Captain R.F. · 57, 69
Ditchburn · 76
Downs, Private C.G. · 45
Dreyer, Lieutenant Colonel Georg · 14

E

Egerton, Sergeant R.E.G. · 45
Eisenhower, General D. D. · 2
Emery, Private R. · 45

F

Ferguson, Private · 70
Finlayson, Lieutenant R. · 17
Foster, Major General Harry · 31
Foster, Private F.E. · 67, 68
Freisen, Corporal J.L. · 45
Fricker, Company Sergeant Major A.A. · 35, 37
Fritz, Lieutenant · 26

G

Galipeau, Sergeant J.A. · 62, 63
Gardipee, Guardsman V.J. · 25
Gartley, Lieutenant K.M. · 35, 36, 45
Geers, family · 36, 44, 64
Geers, farmer · 50
Geers, Janus · 36, 44, 63
Geers, Petrus · 63
Geers, Piet · 64, 90
Geig, Captain · 53
Gelten, family · 63, 97, 98
Gelten, Piet · 79, 80
Gladdines, Jan · 39, 40
Gladdines, Theo · 39
Gordon, Corporal · 24
Gorissen, Arjan · 64
Gorissen, Bart · 53, 64
Gorissen, Christ · 37
Gorissen, family · 53, 64
Gorissen, Janske · 1, 37
Gorissen, Mrs · 63
Gorissen, Tinus · 53, 64
Gove, Sergeant · 63
Graham, J.E. · 41

Griffin, Captain · 53, 70
Gunnarsen, Gunner H.B. · 70

H

Hale, Major · 21
Haszard, Lieutenant Colonel F. · 53
Helmons, Ad · 1, 19, 20, 97, 103
Helmons, family · 23, 50, 51, 78
Helmons, Govert · 90, 91
Helmons, Janus · 65
Herbert, Major, A.R. · 61
Hermus, Mr · 44
Herrington, Captain A. · 43
Hiebert, Private D.H. · 73
Hinton, Lieutenant · 83
Hoendervangers, Piet · 39
Honey, Lance Sergeant H.A. · 67, 68
Hooke, Lieutenant J.C. · 52, 61, 62, 67, 68
Horner, Gunner C.J. · 70
Hudson, Private J.W. · 45
Huijgen, Jan · 64

I

IJzermans, Leen · 54
Iriks, Adriaan · 56
Iriks, family · 56

J

Jewell, Captain J.M. · 55

K

Kearney, Lance Sergeant John · 31
Ketcheson, Sergeant · 24
Kimberly, Sergeant · 24
Koch · 33
Koch, Mr · 50
Koch, Piet · 38
Kock · 37
Kock, Father · 37, 38
Koenraadt, family · 44
Koetsenruyter, Leen · 90
Koll, Sergeant M.R. · 55
Koolen, family · 12, 44, 47, 61
Krijger, Dr · 80

L

Laanen, Toon · 78
Lafontaine, Sergeant J. · 66
Lake, Lieutenant H.E. · 29, 52, 65n
Lambert, Captain H.O. · 71
Lammeree, Piet · 56
Langer, Paratrooper W. · 74
Lavson, Guardsman · 25
Lewis, Major G. · 17
Ligtenberg, Jacobus · 49
Ligtenberg, Jan · 64
Livingstone, Private M.E. · 86, 87
Loos, family · 55

M

MacDougal, Sergeant · 35
MacKinnon, Lieutenant · 32
Maiden, Hank · 30
Martin, Sergeant John · 31
McAdam, Lieutenant A.B. · 51
McInnis, Private · 41
McKergon, Lieutenant · 17
McKillop, Lance-Corporal · 25
McLellan, Gunner A.S. · 55
McLeod, Major J. S. · 33
McPhee, CSM A.R. · 57
Minion, Lance Bombardier D.L. · 55
Moncel, Brigadier R.W. · 18
Montgomery, Field Marshal B.L. · 2
Morrison, Lieutenant F. B. · 31
Muir, Lieutenant · 29
Mulders, Willem · 40
Munro, Ross · 71

N

Neable, Corporal R.C. · 83
Neil, Lieutenant G.E. · 57
Nijssen, family · 22, 51

O

Obre, Bombardier D.E. · 70
Oomen, Father · 37

P

Peart, Lieutenant L. · 33
Peeters, family · 51
Pegelo, Private E.H.J. · 45
Peterson, Private M.A. · 45
Pettit, Sapper H.C. · 86
Phillips, Private G.D. · 68
Pierce, Corporal D.W. · 67
Pope, Lieutenant Colonel · 91
Prophet, Sergeant · 24
Prugh, Captain J.S. · 75

R

Rathbone, Captain · 75
Reid, Company Sergeant Major · 83
Richard, Private F.J. · 40
Riley, Private E.H. · 68
Roberts, Captain R.J. · 35
Roberts, Lieutenant · 52
Rodgers, Gunner N. · 70
Rompf, Private T.S. · 70

S

Schijvenaars, Jan · 53
Scott, Gunner S. · 70
Sills, Gunner W. · 41
Simonds, Lieutenant General G.G. · 3, 6
Sinclair, Captain · 71
Smith, Private L.P. · 69
Smith, Lieutenant Colonel E.M. · 17, 18, 24, 69
Smout, Cornelius · 26
Snoeijers, Mrs · 64
Snoeijers, Piet · 56
Somers, Truusje · 63, 81
Sponheimer, General Otto · 8
Stanley, Corporal J.F. · 88
Stark, Lieutenant D.D. · 73
Stewart, Neil · 30
Stirling · 35
Stirling, Major A.K. · 34, 35, 36, 37, 44, 45, 46, 52
Stock, Captain R.B. · 55
Stockloser, Major B. · 72
Suijkerbuijk, Adriaan · 53, 65

T

Taylor, Private G.K. · 69
Telford, Major · 41
Thicknese, Brigadier · 44
Turner, Private · 83
Turner, Sergeant E.C. · 89

U

Uijtdewilligen, Father · 27

V

van Broekhoven, Christ · 95
van Broekhoven, Louis · 37
van Broekhoven, Toon · 37
van Broekhoven, Willem · 38
van de Ouderaa, Bep · 79, 80
van de Ouderaa, Jan · 79, 80
Van der Heijden, family · 57
van Eekelen, Kees · 14, 39, 57, 65
van Eekelen, Marijn · 38
van Etten, Mayor · 96
van Hooijdonk, family · 81
van Hooijdonk, Jaan · 79
van Hooijdonk, Jan · 79, 80
van Hooijdonk, Piet · 81
van Hooijdonk, Riet · 79
van Kaam, Roel · 27
van Mechelen, brothers · 27
van Mechelen, Henk · 76
van Meer, Jan · 91
van Meer, Koos · 91
van Rooi, Kees · 53
van Rooi, Tinus · 64
van Terheijden, Rikus · 56, 65, 98
Veness, Trooper W.F. · 89
Venus, Lieutenant · 24
Veraart, family · 64
Veraart, Koos · 27, 56
von Zangen, General Gustav-Adolf · 8, 19, 43

W

Waldie, Lieutenant R.G. · 35, 45
Walker, Guardsman · 31
Walton, Guardsman · 31
Weegar, Corporal F.P. · 45

Westman, Guardsman · 25
Weston, Private · 83
Wheeler, Guardsman · 25
Whitbread, Corporal R.C. · 45
Wijnen, family · 64
Wilson, Private A.W. · 45
Wright, Sergeant J.A. · 70

Z

Zimmerman, Lieutenant W.A. · 25, 40

Author Robert Catsburg (left) and Mr Ad Helmons by the war monument on Canadezenweg (Canadians Road) near Welberg. Mr Helmons, 77, lost two brothers to a land mine explosion in November 1944. Having lived all his life in Welberg, he has been the author's chief source of information on local lore and his facilitator for the witness reports that form such an integral part of this book.